TOPSHAM
& SUGAR

CONNECTIONS WITH THE
CARIBBEAN AND VIRGINIA

Published by Topsham Museum
All rights reserved

The moral right of the author has been asserted.

ISBN: 978-1-838-4283-0-3
© Topsham Museum 2021

Designed and typeset by Ned Hoste, The Big Ideas Collective
Printed and bound in Great Britain by CPI UK

TOPSHAM & SUGAR

CONNECTIONS WITH THE CARIBBEAN AND VIRGINIA

a Topsham Museum Research Project
researched and written by
Mike Patrick, Gill McLean and Anna Adcock

Topsham Museum is located in one of a group of late 17th century merchants' houses overlooking the Exe estuary and contains rooms evoking the lifestyle and décor of this period.

The Sail Loft has numerous displays relating to the history of the town and to activities associated with the River Exe, while the River Gallery and walled garden display an important collection of historic boats.

The Museum, which was bequeathed by Dorothy Holman to the community in 1983, includes a section devoted to the actress Vivien Leigh who was at one time married to Dorothy's brother.

Topsham Museum runs a programme of meetings, visits and events throughout the year. Interest in all aspects of local and family history is encouraged using the continually developing resources available in the Local History Room.

The Museum is entirely staffed and run by volunteers, and welcomes all new members as well as offers of help with any aspect of running the Museum.

Further information and the Museum's current opening hours can be found at www.topshammuseum.org.uk.

Contents

Acknowledgements

Much use has been made of records held at the Centre for the Study of the Legacies of British Slavery at University College London.

The authors thank Kamala Nehaul-Harris for advice and encouragement; Gillian Allen for her contributions to Chapter 7; Elizabeth Neill for her contribution to Chapter 9; Crystal Carter for advice on terminology and 'honouring the ancestors'; David Ganpot, the current owner of the Samaritan Great House in Grenada, for permission to use a photograph of the house; Bearnes, Hampton and Littlewood for the photograph of the Barbara Clarke miniature; Catriona Batty for access to the Museum archives; Emma Laws, David Batty and Jenny Pearson for helpful comments on the text.

Foreword

We have a long and well-burnished belief in this country that the transatlantic slave trade was ended by our good offices, and that ultimately the enslaved people of the British Empire were likewise freed through the hard work of William Wilberforce and others, as if enslaved people were only waiting for European benevolence to kick in. We never heard about the uprisings and the resistance; we have avoided the less palatable stories of centuries of the British slave trade, of British plantation owners who benefitted hugely from the labour of enslaved people, of the private and public wealth created out of the despicable treatment of Africans by Europeans. Only quite recently it came as a shock to many of us that slave owners were compensated handsomely from the public purse on the occasion of Abolition. The loans taken out by the British government were finally paid off in 2015. What is more, those formerly enslaved had to continue to perform their former duties for some years as so-called 'apprentices'.

This publication starts from the publicly available records of those who received compensation because they could no longer own human beings, and looks at the lives of families and individuals who lived in or came to Topsham, often to invest their new capital. A fair telling would contrast the stories of plantation owners and those who facilitated the slave economy with those of the people they exploited, but there are no known records describing the experiences of the people enslaved on the plantations discussed in the text. It is therefore inevitably written from a European perspective, but we offer it as a serious contribution to the understanding of real history, as opposed to any kind of mythical narrative that some might prefer.

The starting point for the work was the 'legacies of slave-ownership' database established in 2009 by UCL[1]. We looked at legal and personal papers, local maps and censuses, and records held abroad but accessible online. We have also included a few descriptive extracts from the biographies of Olaudah Equiano (c. 1745-1797), who was captured as a young boy near his home in present-day Nigeria and transported to Barbados; Ottobah Cugoano (c. 1757-c. 1791), kidnapped while playing in a field in what is now Ghana and transported to Grenada; Ashton Warner (1807-1831), born a 'free black' in St Vincent but captured and enslaved there; and Mary Prince (c. 1788-c. 1833), who was born in Bermuda and provided the only known autobiographical account of a female enslaved in the British West Indies[2].

Timeline

1562 John Hawkins' first slave-trading voyage
1627 British colonists arrive in Barbados
1654 Goodrich family patents land in Virginia
1655 Tharp family establishes plantations in Jamaica
1684 Samuel Buttall builds Topsham sugar refinery
1699 *Dragon* sails from Topsham
1715 Baptism and burial in Topsham of Ann Avery
1722 The two 'Black Indian Princes' visit the Exe Estuary
1740s Gibbs family begins trading with Newfoundland and
      the colonies
1765 Samuel Mitchell arrives in Grenada
1771 Isaac Primus buried in Topsham
1783 Abigail Wallay buried in Topsham
1786 Charles Lewis buried, Thomas Greenock baptised,
      in Topsham
1787 Mary and Fanny Wallay baptised in Topsham
1789 Last public sale of an enslaved person in England
1790s Davy family purchases land in Jamaica
1792 Abolition petition signed in Topsham
1805 John Williams buried in Topsham
1807 The sale, barter or transfer of slaves declared illegal in
      the colonies
1809 Mary Williams buried in Topsham
1814 Anti-slavery petition signed in Topsham
1817 William Pennell appointed Consul in Bahia, Brazil
1818 Frederick Sturm, soldier, arrives in Topsham
1833 Slavery Abolition Act passed, to come into effect on
      1 August 1834
1834 Slavery abolished but 'apprenticeship' scheme begins
1837 Thwaites family receives a legacy from John Bolton
      of Liverpool
1838 Slavery finally ends

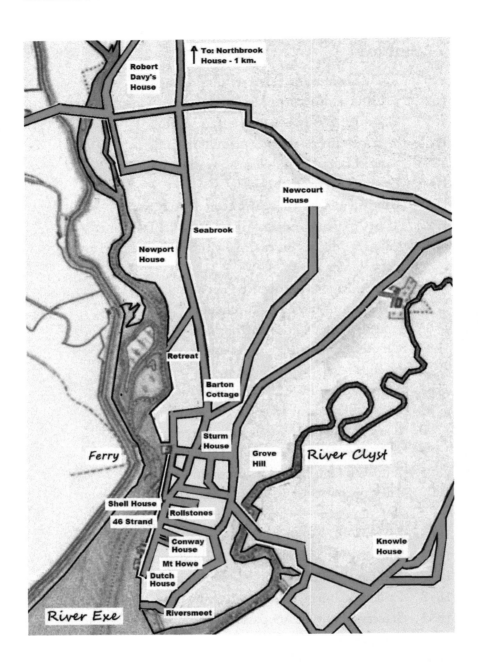

1. The Historical Setting

As Europeans explored tropical and subtropical parts of the Americas in the 16th century, they found they could grow new crops such as tobacco, indigo, rice, cotton and sugar. These all grew prolifically and could be sold readily at home, but the farms were thousands of miles from market and the crops were time-consuming and labour-intensive to grow, harvest and refine. Profitability depended on minimising costs. A small number of workers were willing to relocate to the tropics but they expected wages or grants of land that were deemed unaffordable. Europeans began to look elsewhere for a solution.

During the Middle Ages, the image of West Africa had been one of unlimited wealth: a far-off place of goldmines, metalworkers and legendary empires. Many of the stories were later found to be true. Goods were traded across the Sahara, there was an established university in Timbuktu, and there were sophisticated kingdoms throughout the Sahel and in modern-day Ghana and Nigeria. At the same time, the geography of Africa was not conducive to the development of large-scale farming or industry. With the single exception of camels, indigenous animals could not be domesticated, and while traditional slash-and-burn agriculture suited Africa's low-density population and was ecologically sustainable, it was not scalable for cash crops.

By the 16th century, European maritime expansion allowed ships to reach the West African coast, where merchants found that trade deals could be done. Africa desired manufactured goods, including textiles. In return, local rulers found they had to offer equally valuable and transportable goods that could be produced in quantity. Gold and ivory were available, but not in sufficient amounts. But other kinds of mutually attractive deal could be negotiated.

Africa was culturally and linguistically fragmented, political entities were relatively small and religious variations large. This meant that rulers could be persuaded to bring perceived outsiders from rival tribal groups to the coastal ports, where Europeans could buy them[3]. In Europe, alternative representations of Africans as backward and ungodly were introduced to legitimise this trade. External appearance, and in particular skin colour, became a political and economic tool.

First Portugal and Spain, then Holland and other European countries, began trafficking people from West Africa to work the plantations. Britain's involvement began in 1562. John (later Sir John) Hawkins (1532-1595) sailed from Plymouth, hijacked a Portuguese ship and *got into his possession partly by the sworde and partly by other meanes to the number of 300 negroes.*[4] He took them across the Atlantic and sold them as 'goods' in the Spanish colonies, where they toiled as slaves on the plantations for the rest of their lives. Queen Elizabeth I lent John Hawkins her ship, *Jesus of Lubeck* and over the next six years he made repeated voyages from his base in Plymouth, capturing over 1200 Africans and making profits of up to 50 per cent for his investors.

The Stuart kings were as enthusiastic about this lucrative new business as Elizabeth I had been, and Charles II sent out 'Royal Adventurers' with instructions to buy ivory, gold and people. Shares in their ventures were bought not only by the very rich but also by the middle classes, including the diarist Samuel Pepys (1633-1703). The Adventurers evolved into the Royal African Company (RAC) which operated from a series of forts along the West African coast. Then in 1698, the RAC lost its monopoly and all Englishmen were granted access to the slave trade. The main driver of the trade was sugar. Once people tasted its sweetness in the 1650s, it quickly moved from being a luxury for the rich to a household necessity for the poor. It improved the taste of newly-fashionable coffee, tea and chocolate. It allowed the Navy to replace French brandy with colonial rum as payment for sailors, and it could be used for baking and preserving fruit. The appetite for sugar was insatiable, and tobacco was even more addictive. As demand for these goods rose, so did the demand for enslaved workers.

Barbados was England's first sugar island, with thousands of Africans working on the plantations in worsening conditions. A justification for slavery as a tenet of plantation management was written into the Barbados Slave Code, drawn up by Humphrey Walrond (c. 1602-c. 1669) in 1661. It described Africans as *heathenish brutish and an uncertain and dangerous pride of people* who needed harsh *punishionary Laws for the benefit and good* of the colony. The Code made no mention of reward or duty of care. Instead, fear would be the driver, and whipping and branding were suggested as suitable punishments. Under these laws, white-skinned people could enjoy power, freedom, wealth and long life, and black-skinned people were *chattels to be bought, sold, traded, inherited and serve as collateral for business and debt services.*[5] The life expectancy of an enslaved person was seven years.

Around 1740, as soils in Barbados became depleted, sugar production increased on other islands and the Barbados Slave Code was adopted throughout the Caribbean. Eventually, Jamaica took over as the main source of the sugar brought to England.

While slavery has featured and continues to feature in many cultures and always involves exploitation and coercion, there was a uniquely *special harshness*[6] and inhuman aspect to the transatlantic trade and life on the colonial plantations. Slavery was normalised in the press and in society in general. Euphemisms such as *sugar planter* and *merchant-planter* were coined to legitimise the industry and misrepresent the realities of plantation life. If the general public *ever considered the plight of the African slave, for which there is no evidence, they would have accepted the Catholic* [and Protestant] *Church's acceptance of the commerce, and supposed that it was better for an African to be in the New World at the behest of a Christian master than in Africa working for an infidel.*[7]

Some people invested in the 'triangular trade'. On the first leg of the triangle, ships took goods manufactured in England to Africa to exchange for kidnapped men, women and children. The ensuing three-month voyage across the Atlantic was known as the Middle Passage and the African captives were kept shackled on deck or in the darkness and stench of the hold. On arrival in the Americas, they were taken to slave markets where they were sold to plantation owners, permanently separating parents, children and siblings. Plantation goods, including sugar, coffee, tobacco, spices and indigo, were then loaded as cargo for the voyage home, completing the triangle of trade. One of these slave-trading ships was *Dragon of Topsham*.

Other people bought land or invested in plantations, using enslaved Africans to do the work and exporting the produce back to Britain. It was an easy, if risky, way to make money and operations could be directed locally by hired managers, allowing investors to stay at home and live off the proceeds. *Some owners of enslaved labour amassed vast fortunes, but beneficiaries were also lawyers, doctors, vicars - ordinary people who never set eyes on a plantation or saw an enslaved person or experienced the brutal realities of plantation life.*[8]

It was not even necessary to own or invest in land to benefit from slavery. The plantations were far from European markets, so there was a roaring trade to be done supplying them with farming equipment, manufactured products, food, clothing and conveniences. The large ports of Liverpool, Bristol, Glasgow and London were soon importing and exporting all kinds of goods, and to a much lesser degree smaller ports, including Topsham, also traded with the slave islands. The Topsham Bale Books, for example, record that in 1754 the ships *Mary, Hopewell* and *Cayon* left Topsham for St Kitts and Nevis and *Charming Suckey* was bound for St Lucia. Salt cod from Newfoundland was shipped in barrels to the colonies and used to feed enslaved people, and a number of Topsham fishermen and merchants were involved in that business. Perpetuana, a woollen cloth made in Devon and exported through Topsham, was used to pay tribal chiefs in Africa. The RAC sent more than 3 million yards of perpetuana to Africa, where it was used to make belts from which to hang knives, daggers, purses and keys.[9] Ships were built in Topsham shipyards specifically to trade with the Caribbean, and sugar was refined in a factory in the town.

Slavery helped to shape modern Britain and it has been estimated that the profits of the West Indian plantations created around a shilling in every pound circulating in the British economy in the latter half of the 18th century. As money filtered through many hands, even the wages of the poorest were in part paid from profits of the slavery business.

Throughout the Caribbean, the enslaved population tried desperately to free themselves. There were rebellions in St Lucia between 1795 and 1797, in Saint-Domingue (now Haiti and the Dominican Republic) after 1793 and Guadeloupe in 1802. Multi-class rebellions involving both enslaved people and free people of mixed heritage took place in Grenada and St Vincent in 1795 and in Curaçao in 1800.

In Britain, just a few lone voices were prepared to speak out at first, but gradually the movement to abolish the slave trade increased, led by Quakers and other non-conformists. Public opinion gradually changed.

In 1772, a court case case brought an important change in the law. An enslaved man called James Somerset was brought to England. He escaped, was recaptured and an attempt was made to force him aboard a ship to Jamaica. The Lord Chief Justice ruled that James Somerset could not be taken by force and that while he was in England, he was a free man. That meant that once an enslaved African set foot on English soil, they could not be owned by another person. This was a major change, but the law was not always adhered to and some black people, as in the unsuccessful attempt on James Somerset, were pressed aboard ships and returned to the colonies. There were also clandestine sales of enslaved people on the quaysides and in the coffee houses of the major ports. The last public sale of a black person in England was in Liverpool in 1789.

Logo designed for Anti-Slavery Society by Josiah Wedgwood in 1787

In 1774, John Wesley (1703-1791) wrote an influential pamphlet castigating the slave trade and slavery. In 1787, Ottobah Cugoano self-published his autobiography and publicly demanded total abolition, and the emancipation of all slaves.[10] The memoirs of Olaudah Equiano were published two years later and widely read, and the life story of Toussaint Louverture (1743-1803), a revolutionary leader in Haiti, was also circulated. William Wilberforce (1759-1833), MP for Hull, took on political leadership of the movement for abolition and the following year a committee of the Privy Council was set up to investigate the slave trade.

Eventually, from 1 May 1807, the *sale, barter, or transfer of slaves* was made illegal in British colonies. By that time, 3.1 million people had been shipped across the Atlantic by the British to work on their plantations. Although the Act ended the buying and selling of Africans, it did not abolish the practice of slavery itself and there was a self-sustaining population of 775,000 enslaved people in the British Caribbean, and over four million in the southern states of America.

In the years after 1807, hopes that ending further slave shipments would lead to improvements in the circumstances of those already enslaved were dashed, and pressure for emancipation steadily grew. There were more petitions and public meetings, including one in Topsham.

News of changes in the public mood came not only to the ears of the planters in the colonies, but as rumours to the enslaved people themselves, raising expectations of freedom and leading to rebellions in Barbados in 1816, Demerara in 1823 and Jamaica in 1831. Each of these rebellions was noted for trying to restrict action to the destruction of buildings and sugar cane fields, showing a determination to avoid killing or injuring white people.

Black people living in Britain, such as Frederick Douglass (1817-1895) who had escaped from slavery in Maryland, toured the country to give eyewitness accounts of conditions on the plantations and to campaign for abolition. Douglass was a talented orator, who by his own example counteracted the argument that enslaved people lacked the intellectual ability to function as independent citizens. The memoirs of Ashley Warner and Mary Prince were published.[11] Mary Prince's account particularly influenced female campaigners as it highlighted the break-up of families, the absence of normal married life and the brutal working conditions and savage beatings endured by girls and women enslaved on the plantations.

In 1833, Parliament received over 5000 anti-slavery petitions, together containing almost 1.5 million signatures. A bill was passed that would emancipate nearly 800,000 British colonial slaves the following year.

> *But property and the right to property ran at the very heart of British culture and British law. Slaveholders claimed that emancipation amounted to confiscation of their property. This amounted to an assault on their legal rights to own property and could also devastate the British economy. The abolitionists were forced to abandon their most fundamental and cherished principle and acknowledge that enslaved people were property and that therefore slaveholders could be compensated, in order to achieve their goal of ending slavery. Emancipation could only be achieved if it was linked to compensation.*[12]

On 1 August 1834, when slavery was finally abolished in most of the British colonies, no restitution was offered to any of the 800,000 enslaved people who laboured there. No apology was offered to the 12 million Africans who had been trafficked by the European powers in the holds of slave ships, nor to the two million who died before reaching their destination. No mention was made of the trafficked people's children and grandchildren who were born into slavery and worked all their lives in the fields and homes of European colonists.

Instead, the government used 40 per cent of its national budget to compensate the slave owners for their lost 'property'. There was an immediate scramble for the money, and claims and counter-claims were laboriously checked and recorded by government officials in London.

Only children under six years old were granted immediate freedom. Everyone else had to serve an unpaid period of 'apprenticeship', initially set at 12 years, but later reduced to four.[13] The Governor of Jamaica issued a proclamation to the 'apprentices'. House servants were enjoined *to serve* [their] *masters with cheerfulness, and with the gratitude they deserve.*

Field workers were told, *your master must give you clothes, provision grounds, and medical attendance if you are sick. I hope you will give him cheerfully and willingly the very small portion of your time which* [he] *is entitled to.*[14]

Under the new employment terms, masters or overseers were not permitted to strike 'apprentices' or put them in the stocks, and they could only be punished by order of a special magistrate.[15] However, the new laws were frequently ignored.

Even after 1838, when the 'apprentices' were free to join the job market, most of the available work was on the very same plantations the people had worked on as slaves. Wages were low, there was limited representation on legislatures and few opportunities to buy land, start businesses or form new communities. The new systems were frequently abused, with forced labour and flogging in prisons.

In the years following emancipation, plantation owners found it was impossible to compete with sugar produced by enslaved workers in South America, Cuba and mainland North America, while in Europe, local beet-sugar also became available. Many plantation owners cut their losses and returned to Britain. Others decided to stick it out and some colonies, particularly Trinidad, Tobago and Guyana, brought in indentured workers from India and China.

Gradually, bananas replaced sugar as the major plantation crop and colonial governments reformed the judiciary, education and healthcare. Roads and railways were built, and water supplies and sanitation improved. The white propertied class still held dominant political positions, though, and the black population remained poor and disenfranchised. Emigration was substantial throughout the 20th century and today the Caribbean islands are dependent on cash crops and tourism. Much of the soil is depleted and prone to erosion and the region is extremely vulnerable to climate change. Parallel experiences as plantation colonies have given the region a strong identity and largely common culture, blending African, Asian, European and native American influences.

2. The Voyage of *Dragon of Topsham*

Topsham's first and only certain involvement in the triangular trade involved a ship called *Dragon of Topsham* in 1699.

By the end of the 17th century, the demand for slave labour was such that the Royal African Company could no longer meet its commitments, and a year before *Dragon* set sail its trading monopoly came to an end. All Englishmen were granted the right to trade in slaves upon payment of a 10 per cent 'affiliation fee' and many private businessmen seized the opportunity to invest. Amongst them were *Dragon's* owners: Arthur Jeffry, Joseph Anthony, William Penneck and Martha Broderick, all from Exeter; Robert Corker of Falmouth; and the ship's captain Christopher Butcher. Records show that in that single year of 1699, almost 39,000 Africans were forced aboard European slaving ships bound for the Americas.[16]

Ships were usually adapted for use as slavers and *Dragon,* a 60-ton vessel equipped with six guns,[17] may have been refitted in a Topsham shipyard. A 3m high *barricado*, made of wood and topped with spikes and guns, would have been constructed to divide the deck, allowing captured men to be chained together and shackled to the decking in the forward part of the ship, while the crew remained behind the *barricado* with the captured women and children.

Dragon sailed from Topsham on 4 March 1699, early enough in the season to avoid the threat of pirates. The cargo was not made up of the usual bolts of woollen perpetuanas or Indian cotton, nor the guns that changed the balance of power in Africa and destroyed traditional societies. Instead, the hold contained a more general assortment of trade goods: 3 tons (159 bars) of Swedish iron, 15 cwt gunpowder, 4 cwt wrought pewter, 2 cwt ironmonger wares, 1½ cwt tapseils (cheap cotton), some stone pots, 56 lb shoes, 3 dozen felt hats with bands, 1 dozen worsted stockings, 23 dozen corn necklaces with coral, 1 chest of glasses and glassware, 1 hogshead of aqua vitae, 56 gross of tobacco pipes, and an unspecified quantity of cut and rolled tobacco.

A rapid 21-day passage brought *Dragon* to the mouth of the Gambia River where the Royal African Company had a trading post, just one of the string of forts from Morocco in the north to the Cape of Good Hope in the south. In 1699, the entire West African coastline was known as the 'Guinea Coast' and the sole purpose of the company's trading posts was to exchange cloth, metals, guns, cutlery and trinkets for silver, ivory, and the most lucrative commodities, gold and slaves.

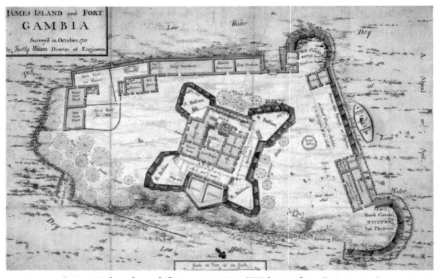

James Island and fort in 1755 (Wikimedia Commons)

In London, the gold was minted as one-inch coins containing ¼ ounce of gold, with the king's head on one side and an elephant (the Royal African Company symbol, sometimes combined with a castle) on the reverse. To reflect their origin, the coins were known as 'Guineas' and their value, initially fluctuating with the price of gold, eventually settled at 21 shillings.

On arrival at the Gambia River at the end of March, *Dragon* anchored near the RAC fort on James Island. This was a centre of the RAC's activities, second only to the infamous Cape Coast Castle, further south in modern Ghana. A network of African middle-men, called *caboceers*,[18] obtained captives from local warlords and walked them from the hinterland to the coast.

> *Their way of bringing them is, tying them by the Neck with Leather-Thongs, at about a yard distance from each other, 30 or 40 in a String, having generally a Bundle of Corn or an Elephant's Tooth upon each of their Heads . . . Merchants who follow this Trade . . . go up into the Inland Country with the Goods, which they buy from the White Men, and with them purchasing in various Countries Gold, Slaves, and Elephant Teeth.*[19]

When they arrived at the fort, the captives (adults and children) were immediately branded on their chests with the RAC initials. They were kept in separate male and female dungeons, perhaps for months on end, until a ship bound for Virginia or the Caribbean could be filled. In the fort and during the voyage, sexual exploitation was a regular part of the intimidation process.

The RAC agent on the Gambia River was Thomas Corker, the brother of *Dragon* shareholder Robert Corker. At first, he was slow to provide captives to fill *Dragon's* hold, so Captain Butcher threatened to up-anchor and sail south to another fort on the Sherbro river estuary in Sierra Leone. While negotiations were proceeding, Christopher Butcher succumbed to disease, probably malaria. He died in the middle of June and command passed to the first mate, Henry Taylor.

Eventually, the crew loaded 57 Africans aboard *Dragon*, together with two of the commodities particularly associated with the Gambia region:[20] ivory (10 kentels or cwt) and beeswax (14 kentels). It was a modest haul for the investors, especially as 29 of the captives were shipped on behalf of Agent Corker at £3 10s a head.

Departure from James Island was delayed by a lack of provisions and contrary winds and the enslaved Africans made a bid for freedom. This cost the lives of two crewmen and seven of the captives. When the crew opened fire, two African men were killed immediately. Five others decided their only option was to commit suicide and they leaped overboard, still bound to each other by chains.

Olaudah Equiano
(c. 1745-1797)

Dragon finally sailed with 50 African captives, bound for the English colony of Barbados, 4800 km away. The Middle Passage took around 80 days, and the Africans would have been shackled together, on deck during the day and below-deck at night, and fed minimal rations of rice, beans and bread together with two pints of water. On a typical voyage, one in every six became sick and died.

Olaudah Equiano was about ten years old when he was taken from present-day Nigeria to Barbados. Later, he recalled:[21]

I was soon put down under the decks, and there I received such a salutation in my nostrils as I had never experienced in my life: so that, with the loathsomeness of the stench, and crying together, I became so sick and low that I was not able to eat ... on my refusing to eat, one of them [the crew] held me fast by the hands and laid me across the windlass, and tied my feet, while the other flogged me severely. Many a time we were near suffocation from the want of fresh air, being deprived thereof for days together. This, and the stench of the necessary tubs, carried off many.

Dragon reached Barbados late in September 1699 with 43 of the kidnapped people still alive. Of these, just 14 were delivered for the investors of the voyage (the others had been carried on behalf of Agent Corker). They were consigned to local merchant Joseph Hole with the ivory, beeswax and remaining goods loaded at Topsham but not sold on the Guinea Coast.

The degrading and horrific sale of the African people on the quay in Barbados would have been incomprehensible and utterly degrading. One of the Africans from the *Dragon* died during the sale. For the others, it marked the beginning of a brutal new existence. Olaudah

Equiano wrote of the sale he endured on arrival in Barbados:[22]

> *On a signal given (as the beat of a drum) the buyers rush at once into the yard where the slaves are confined, and make choice of that parcel they like best ... In this manner, without scruple, are relations and friends separated, most of them never to see each other again. ... O ye nominal Christians ... Is it not enough that we are torn from our country and friends, to toil for your luxury and avarice? ... Why are parents to lose their children, brothers their sisters, or husbands their wives?*

Acting-Captain Henry Taylor later claimed that his crew had all died and that he had lain at death's door in Barbados for eight months. Meanwhile, on 25 December 1699, the investors wrote to him:

> *We are also very uneasy for want of a Letter from you to give us Some Light what was done on the Coast of Guinny and in the whole Course of the Voyage ... the cargo we sent out from hence cost us above £500 & to hear of but 14 Slaves for our Account aboard which could not cost above £100 is astonishing.*

The investors assumed that the purchase of 14 enslaved people *could not have cost above £100,* that is, £7 per person. They clearly expected that £7 would buy the life and perpetual labour of an African man and all his descendants. At home, £7 would have bought just eight months' work by an agricultural labourer.[23] And to further put it into perspective, Henry Taylor later sued the consortium for his own unpaid wages of £6 *per month.*

It was 1703 before Taylor reached England and within a fortnight he was arrested. The warrant complained that he had not acted according to his duties or orders as he:

> *... hath applyed the said Ship and her Cargo ... to his owne use or wasted and destroyed or wilfully cast the same away & hath not given the Owners any Account thereof.*

For *Dragon's* owners, the shipping of enslaved Africans was morally indistinguishable from shipping any other saleable goods and the wording, repulsive to us today, treats ivory, felt hats with bands, and enslaved people equally – all part of the *Cargo … wasted* by Taylor.

Henry Taylor never again shipped out for the coast of Guinea. Of the investors, only Robert Corker surmounted his losses from the voyage, mounting one more slaving venture and becoming the leading Cornish merchant of his day.

There are no further records of the 42 African people trafficked to Barbados aboard the *Dragon* and purchased by planters to work the sugar plantations.

A further aspect of the relationship between the Royal African Company and the people of Africa can be seen in the treatment of two young men who were brought to England from Delagoa (in modern-day Mozambique) at the behest of their father, a local chieftain. They were presented at Court, instructed in the Christian religion and baptised James Chandos Mastoon and John Twogood Mastoon in Twickenham in June 1721. This 'hospitality' was not unusual: both the RAC and its associate the East India Company[24] had policies of entertaining, and even educating, children of selected potentates in order to forge closer and more profitable links between English traders and local influencers.

In 1722, the Society for Promoting Christian Knowledge wanted the young men to be returned to Delagoa, along with missionaries to further the spread of the Christian faith. According to a report in the *London Journal,* Marmaduke Penwell was appointed as missionary, having received a fee of £500 from the East India Company.[25]

In April 1722, they embarked on the Royal African Company ship *Northampton* under the command of John Sharrow.[26] The weather took a turn for the worse and Captain Sharrow ran for the mouth of the Exe. Unfortunately, while going over Topsham bar, *Northampton* grounded heavily and damaged her hull. Prince James became frightened and Captain Sharrow immediately wrote to London. The RAC merely advised him to:

> *use all the fair means you can to reduce him to quietness and ease, having at the same time a regard to yourselves & the safety & success of your voyage.*

Northampton put to shore for repairs and on 1 May the missionary Marmaduke Penwell recorded in his diary that he discovered the ship's captain severely beating James. Penwell seemed less concerned about the abuse than about the injustice of the captain's subsequent name-calling:

As soon as he saw me [Penwell], *he called me a Presbyterian rogue.*[27]

According to another entry in Penwell's journal, on 4 May Prince James left the inn where they were staying and hanged himself by his own garters from an apple tree in a nearby garden. The location of the inn is not known, but it may well have been somewhere in Topsham. It was suggested at the time that Prince James had been *in a phrenzy* and perhaps had had a quarrel with his brother. He was buried ashore and the RAC remained unperturbed:

> *the violent death of Prince James ... was what might have been expected from his late behaviour ... it is certainly very happy that Prince John (to whom pay my humble services) keeps his Temper, it makes Amends for the Loss of the other who was a Wretch whose being was not to be regarded nor his Death lamented.*

This shabby episode sums up the division between the concerned public stance of the RAC towards the two princes and the private reality that the company considered all Africans to be expendable.

As a footnote, the *Northampton* departed after repairs and eventually delivered Prince John to Delagoa. According to Penwell's journal, Prince John then went to his mother's house and shut the door in the missionary's face. The prince emerged after six hours but gave Penwell *such frowns and looked so surly upon him* that Penwell returned immediately to the ship and sailed back to England.

3. The Sugar House: *The Buttall Family*

Topsham's earliest known connection with the plantation owners of the Caribbean began around the 1680s.

Half a century earlier earlier, in 1627, the first 50 British settlers had arrived in Barbados. Some were indentured workers lured by the promise of land grants on completion of five-year contracts. There were also 10 Africans who had been captured from a Portuguese slaving ship encountered on the voyage from England. The Barbados settlers initially planted tobacco, cotton and indigo and soon began planting sugar. The economics of using enslaved people rather than indentured workers immediately became clear and during the 1630s, 20,000 Africans were transported from the Guinea Coast to Barbados. By 1700, almost a quarter of a million newly-enslaved people had disembarked onto the island. *Barbados was the first* [Caribbean] *slave society, built and sustained entirely on the enslavement of Africans with no alternative form of economic development.*[28]

The Mill Yard, Antigua 1823 (British Library Collection)

One of the few accounts of life as an enslaved person in the Caribbean was reported to anti-slavery campaigners in London by Ashton Warner, who had been enslaved on a sugar plantation in St Vincent in the 1820s:[29]

> [The workers] *were obliged to be in the field before five o'clock in the morning; and, as the negro houses were at the distance of from three to four miles from the cane pieces, they were, generally, obliged to rise as early as four o'clock, to be at their work in time. The driver is first in the field and calls the slaves together by cracking the whip or blowing the conch shell. ... if any of the slaves are so unfortunate as to be too late, even by a few minutes ... the driver flogs them as they come in, with the cart-whip, or with a scourge of tamarind rods. When flogged with the whip, they are stripped and held down upon the ground, and exposed in the most shameful manner.*

> *In the cultivation of the canes the slaves work in a row. Each person has a hoe, and the women are expected to do as much as the men ... They work from five o'clock to nine, when they are al-lowed to sit down for half an hour in the field ... after half an hour's respite* [they] *labour till twelve o'clock ... They are allowed two hours of mid-day intermission ... During this interval every slave must pick a bundle of grass to bring home for the cattle at night. The grass grows in tufts, often scattered over a great space of ground. ... I have frequently known them occupied the whole two hours in collecting it. They work again in gang from two till seven o'clock. It is then dark ... The overseer ... demands of every man and woman their bundles of grass ... if it be too light, the person who presents it is either instantly laid down and flogged severely with the cart-whip, or is put into the stocks for the whole night.*

During the harvesting season the regime was even harsher. The production of sugar involved cutting canes by hand and crushing them in a water- or wind-powered sugar mill to express the juice, and this took place in the closing months of the year. After cutting, speed was needed to avoid spoilage, so the mills worked non-stop and a 24-

hour shift system operated. Feeding the canes into the crushers was hard and dangerous work and serious accidents were not uncommon. The sugar juice was then piped into cisterns where it was boiled and refined. It crystallised as it cooled and the workers shovelled it into earthenware moulds or wooden hogsheads. After about a month they emptied the moulds and the crudely refined muscovado sugar was ready.[30]

There was duty to be paid on refined sugar, so it was shipped as brown, muscovado sugar and then refined into saleable white sugar once it was safely landed in Britain. Shipping began early in the New Year and continued until July and the onset of the hurricane season.

Three brothers, Jonathon, Samuel and Charles Buttall, the sons of a blacksmith from Wrexham, saw an opportunity to become involved in that trade.

The youngest brother Charles (1644-1694) emigrated to Barbados and acquired a sugar plantation of 48 acres where he had 43 enslaved workers and an overseer. *Buttal's,*[31] in the parish of St George's, is marked on maps to this day. Charles Buttall married and prospered,[32] and in 1694 was elected a Member of the Barbados Assembly. When his widow Mary died in 1718 she left her property, which included the enslaved people, to the Alleyne and Peers families into which her daughters had married:

> *I Mary Buttall of the Island of Barbados give and bequeath unto my two grandsons Thomas Alleyne and Henry Peers Jr all the Land commonly called Morgans to be equally divided between them. I give and bequeath unto my grandson Thomas Alleyne a Negro Boy by name Pompy which usually waited on me. I give and bequeath unto my granddaughter Elizabeth Peers a Negro girl by name Caddo. Lastly, I give and bequeath unto my Loving daughter Elizabeth Alleyne all the Negroes of my own Purchase.*

The other two Buttall brothers remained at home in England and set up sugar businesses here. Jonathon (d.1695), built a sugar bakery at Battersea in London.

Samuel (1641-1723) leased land in Carolina in June 1682, perhaps becoming the absentee landlord of a plantation, and at home he built sugar refineries in Plymouth and at the north end of Topsham near the present-day motorway bridge. He purchased six acres of land alongside the River Exe comprising two fields, *lying and being near to Goodman's well in the parish of Topsham including Goodman's Well Rock, hedges outside and the waste ground as well as all Edifices.*[33] By 1707, the refinery was fully operational and described as *a convenient sugar house with the necessary utensils for the refining of sugar.* In 1717, 3606 cwt of sugar was imported from Barbados into Exeter[34] and some at least was likely to have been refined at Topsham.

Samuel's son Humphrey inherited the Plymouth refinery and at Topsham, Samuel went into partnership with two other sons, Benjamin and Charles. In 1718, he invested £2100, Benjamin £2109 and Charles £1575. These were significant amounts, equivalent to millions today.

As the woollen cloth trade declined in Devon, some cloth merchants branched out into trading with North America and the Caribbean. William Upcott from Tiverton:[35]

> *did purchase a dwelling house with cellars or warehouses at Topsham[36] commodious for carrying on a joint trade in partnership with his father John Upcott ... and did go with part of his family to Topsham for sundry reasons and amongst others to forward and receive goods and merchandizes.*

Initially trading with Carolina, the Upcotts diversified into the Barbados sugar trade. During a voyage in April 1726, their ship *Charles Town* sailed to Barbados with an outward cargo of 400 pieces of serge, 2262 yards of Irish linen, 9000 ells of narrow German linen (a coarse material used to clothe enslaved people) and some canvas. The ship returned that October with 600 cwt of muscovado sugar, 25 cwt of white sugar, 36 cwt of ginger and materials (presumably indigo) for use in dyeing cloth. On arrival at their quay in Topsham, Upcott's sugar could well have been taken by small ship or lighter to the Buttalls' Topsham refinery and once refined sold inland to local sugar bakers and grocers.

On Samuel Buttall's death in 1723, his widow Mary inherited his share of the Topsham sugar house and the 1000 acres of registered land in Carolina.[37] Soon, a notice was placed in the *London Gazette* by Mary Buttall and a son, John. While there is no evidence the property was actually let the advert contains a useful description of the facilities:[38]

> *To be let, a complete Sugar-house, 80 foot long, 40 foot broad [slightly bigger than a tennis court] and 7 stories high, with Warehouse, a Distil-House, with Backs for working Mollasses, &c. situate in Topsham, about 5 Miles from Exon, by the River side, where a Ship of 80 Tons can come to be unloaded by a Crane fixed for that purpose; to which belongs a Dwelling-House 3 Rooms on a Floor, 4 Story high, encompassed by large Gardens, and an Orchard stock'd with the best of Fruit Trees, &c. wall'd all round; a Brewhouse, Stables, Coach-house, and a Barn, with 7 Acres of Meadow Land adjoining. Enquiries of Mrs. Mary Buttall in Exon; or at Mr. John Buttall's in Tower-Street. N.B. All the above Premises were and did belong to Mr. Samuel Buttall of that Place lately deceased.*

Mary Buttall died in 1730 and the refinery at Topsham passed to her sons, Benjamin and John. John, who had been apprenticed to a lorimer (a maker of bits and spurs) in London, had no interest in sugar refining and his half share passed to his sister, Mary Hodges, who appears to have mismanaged her investments. To complicate matters, Benjamin owed her £612 and she in turn owed her son-in-law, Exeter physician Dr Thomas Glass (1709-1786), some £1800. By 1742, the Topsham sugar house was described as being *in a state of decay and void for the lack of a tenant.*[39]

In 1756 John Eliot visited Topsham and in a letter to his uncle made a reference to current events, writing of certain *Cellars by the Dock being let to one Dr Glass who hires them for sugar pans, his Sugar house betwixt this place and Exeter being taken by the Government for the reception of French prisoners.*[40]

It was not until after the death of Mary Hodges in 1744 that the finances were resolved. Her share of the sugar house was sold,[41] and eventually in 1766 it was assigned to Dr Thomas Glass in settlement of debts. Benjamin Buttall (b.1743), a Topsham master mariner who had inherited the other half share of the property, assigned that, too, to Thomas Glass forever.[42]

In 1769, three years after Dr Glass took full control of the sugar house, the remains of the estate were sold *with the utensils and implements used in a sugar bakery still remaining on the premises,*[43] to Robert Orme (c.1725-1790) for £940.

This sum represents the last evidence of proceeds from the Buttall sugar refinery business. It is not known what eventually happened to Samuel Buttall's estate in Carolina.

The present-day house, *The Retreat,* was built on the site around 1770. Many remains of sugar moulds have been found in the grounds, and some are on display at the Royal Albert Memorial Museum in Exeter.

These sugar moulds are a reminder of Topsham's links to sugar produced by enslaved people in Barbados but refined in Topsham for the exclusive use of people in Britain.

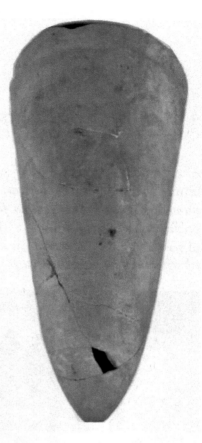

Conical sugar mould

4. The Gentleman's Residence: *The Hamiltons*

After purchasing the Buttall sugar house in 1769, Robert Orme immediately built *The Retreat*, described as *an elegant villa with numerous apartments elegantly furnished, and with useful offices at a proper distance from the house.* There were good gardens and 30 acres of pasture adjoining, as well as *a small pavilion with 3 bedchambers, a library and a hot and cold bath.*[44]

A VIEW of the HOUSE of ROBERT ORME ESQ. near Topsham in Devon

The Retreat, by an unknown artist – the seven-storey sugar-house can still be seen to the right (courtesy DHC)

Robert Orme died in 1790, having already sold *The Retreat* to Alexander Hamilton (1732-1809), a member of a well-known Scottish family from Salcoats on the Ayrshire coast. He had already made a fortune by the 1780s when he retired to Devon. He rapidly entered public life and in 1786 he served as High Sheriff for the county.[45] That same year he was knighted by George III for congratulating the king on his escape from an assassination attempt.[46]

As well as owning land and property in Devon, Sir Alexander owned a plantation with over 100 enslaved workers on the Caribbean island of Grenada. He had inherited the Samaritan estate from his brother Dr Robert Hamilton (b.1738), who emigrated in 1776 and died without male heirs. The estate was in the parish of St Patrick in the north of Grenada and comprised 285 acres[47] of sugar and cocoa, and a sugar refinery powered by a watermill.

As an absentee plantation owner, Sir Alex's affairs were represented by a local attorney. It is unlikely that he ever visited his property, over 3000 miles away by sea, and would have known of its affairs only by written reports and by reference to his considerable financial returns.

A contemporary account of life on a sugar plantation in Grenada was written by Ottobah Cugoano in 1787:

> *seeing my miserable companions often cruelly lashed, and, as it were, cut to pieces, for the most trifling faults; this made me often tremble and weep, but I escaped better than many of them. For eating a piece of sugar-cane, some were cruelly lashed, or struck over the face, to knock their teeth out. Some told me they had their teeth pulled out, to deter others, and to prevent them from eating any cane in future. Thus seeing my miserable companions and countrymen in this pitiful, distressed, and horrible situation, with all the brutish baseness and barbarity attending it, could not but fill my little mind with horror and indignation.*

> *Thanks be to God, I was delivered from Grenada, and that horrid brutal slavery. A gentleman coming to England took me for his servant, and brought me away, where I soon found my situation become more agreeable.*

At home in Topsham, Sir Alexander set about making improvements to his new home, as described by the artist Swete in 1792, during one of his painting tours:

> *Having landed, I rode to the Retreat where I breakfasted. This is now an excellent house, which with the addition of an attic storey, has received vast improvements from the hands of the present proprietor. The gardens, offices, greenhouse and greater part of the beautiful shrubberies have been raised by him and there are few more elegant or comfortable seats in the country.[48]*

The Retreat, Rev. Swete 1792 (courtesy DHC)

Hamilton also acquired considerable amounts of land in Topsham and adjacent parishes, and effectively operated as Lord of the Manor. Over 200 years later, a road in Topsham is called Hamilton Road and a riverside path is still known as *Sir Alex Walk*.

His business interests were wide-ranging and in 1800 he bought the *Henry Addington*, an East Indiaman operated by the East India Company which made five trading voyages to the Far East under his ownership.

The Henry Addington, *West India Docks 1802 (Wikimedia Commons)*

Purchase of the ship and ongoing investment costs may have been partly funded by profits from the plantation in Grenada.

Sir Alexander decided to leave most of his wealth to the eldest son of his sister Mary Kelso (b.1744), under the condition that his heir formally changed his surname from Kelso to Hamilton. By 1809, when Sir Alexander died and was buried in Topsham, two of his sister's sons had also died, and by coincidence the surviving son had been christened Alexander Hamilton Kelso (1783-1853).

A notice in *The London Gazette* explained the situation:

> *Whitehall, March 23, 1811 - His Royal Highness the Prince Regent has been graciously pleased, in the Name and on the Behalf of His Majesty, to give and grant unto Alexander Hamilton Kelso, Esq, … His Majesty's Royal Licence and Authority that he and his Issue may … assume and take the Surname of Hamilton only, and also bear the Arms of Hamilton, quarterly, in the first Quarter, with the Arms of Kelso; such Arms being … recorded in the Herald's Office.*[49]

The new Alexander Hamilton Hamilton, aged 26, was in the south of India, working for the East India Company. He returned to England and moved into *The Retreat*. He took control of the family estate around Topsham and in 1828 he was appointed Deputy Lieutenant of Devonshire.[50] He also became the third member of his family to own the Samaritan cocoa plantation in Grenada, with its 100 or so enslaved workers.

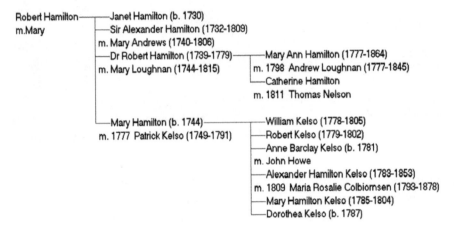

Hamilton family tree

The Great House, Samaritan Estate (probably occupied by the estate overseer)

From around this time, plantation owners were required to conduct censuses and to submit them to the Office for the Registry of Colonial Slaves. On Samaritan, as on most estates, the number of people enslaved fell gradually after 1807, when the transatlantic trade was abolished and numbers could no longer be replenished simply by purchasing additional workers from the trading ships.

Year	Slaves	Male	Female	Attourney	Proprietor
1817	128	63	65	Andrew Houstoun	A.H. Hamilton
1822	110	50	60	Geo. Paterson	A.H. Hamilton
1825	113	57	56	Andrew Houstoun	A.H. Hamilton
1828	110	55	55	Andrew Houstoun	A.H. Hamilton
1829	109	54	55	Andrew Houstoun	A.H. Hamilton
1833	102	48	54	Geo. Paterson	A.H. Hamilton
1834	38	22	16	Geo. Paterson	A.H. Hamilton

Register of slaves on the Samaritan Estate in the parish of St Patrick's, Grenada (Annual profits from the plantation are not recorded)

Following his uncle's example, Alexander H. Hamilton ran the Samaritan Estate as an absentee landlord, using management by well-known attorneys George Paterson (d.1852), sometime Governor of Grenada, and Hon. Andrew Houstoun of Jordanhill, Glasgow (1779-1830).

There were established links between the Houstoun family and the Topsham elite. In 1802, Andrew Houstoun's younger brother Robert had married Frances Caplain Follett (1788-1864) of the celebrated Topsham family. Robert Houstoun (1780-1862) was a soldier in India and like Alexander Hamilton, he was the absentee owner of plantations in Grenada.

In 1834, when slavery was abolished, Alexander Hamilton applied for compensation from the British Government for the loss of his inherited 'property', the 102 people enslaved on the Samaritan plantation. In November 1835, he was awarded £3,784 15s 3d. The enslaved workers themselves received no compensation and had to work four years of unpaid apprenticeship before they were finally granted freedom.

Robert Houstoun was awarded £15,375 11s 5d for the loss of 603 workers enslaved on his four estates in Grenada, and some of this benefit would have passed to his six children.

In Topsham, the Hamiltons continued in their role of landed gentry and benevolent gentlemen. A certain amount of the compensation money was passed on to the Topsham community in charitable acts and there were generous contributions to the upkeep of the church. The death of Alexander Hamilton Hamilton was recorded in the *Western Times* with the following comment:

> ... *his time spent in retirement was devoted to the daily exercise of every Christian grace; humble and devout, his piety was sincere; his charity was large, without ostentation, even unbounded. In him the poor have lost a kind and generous benefactor, and to those who had known brighter days, his hand was ever ready gladly to distribute of that wealth of which the providence of God had made him, in his own estimation, the unworthy steward.*[51]

The newspaper refers to Hamilton's wealth as 'the providence of God' and there is no mention of the endless toil of hundreds of people in Grenada.

The Retreat continued in the ownership of the Hamilton family until the death of Alexander Kelso Hamilton in 1929, and the property was sold in 1931. The garden and coach house subsequently became a boat yard and by 1938 the house had been converted into five flats.

On the Samaritan plantation in Grenada, Indian workers from Calcutta were employed in 1857 to make up for labour shortages following emancipation of the slaves. By the late 1800s the estate had been sold. The Great House was restored in 2001 and is now a private house with the original cocoa building and just six acres of land. In 2007, the racing driver Lewis Hamilton was able to trace his roots back to some of those who had toiled for the benefit of the Hamilton family on the Samaritan estate.

5. From Grenada to Newport House:
The Mitchells

Samuel Mitchell (1750-1805), like Alexander Hamilton, made money from the Caribbean plantations and then retired to Topsham. He was born on 5 October 1750 at Barge Yard, Bucklersbury, a middle-class street in central London,[52] the eldest son of Thomas and Elizabeth Mitchell. He was baptised by his grandfather, Rev. Samuel Chandler (1693-1766), a Presbyterian minister, bookseller and Fellow of the Royal Society.

Nothing is known of Samuel Mitchell's childhood, but as a boy in an academic family it is likely that he received a good education. As a young adult, he chose to seek his fortune as a sugar planter in Grenada. The island had only recently been acquired from the French[53] and Samuel may have been lured by a pamphlet published in the 1760s[54] which attractively advertised Grenada as:

> *full of large mountains forming several fertile valleys and producing a great number of fine rivulets, which facilitate the construction of water mills for the use of sugar plantations.*

In such a place a bright, middle-class boy could do well. Adventure and social advancement beckoned.

Samuel joined a tight-knit community of British merchants and planters. Dr Robert Hamilton bought the Samaritan Estate in the north of the island in 1776, and with a white community of only a few hundred people, it is likely that they were acquainted.

Little is known of Mitchell's early career. He may have acted as an overseer or factor (estate manager), but he must have built a solid reputation as he later rose to great prominence, in spite of a remittent fever causing enlargement of his spleen. An estate hospital nurse advised that the complaint, common among local children, could be relieved by kneading the spleen. While Mitchell was helped by this treatment, the problem never left him.[55]

James Baillie and family c. 1784, Thomas Gainsborough
(Wikimedia Commons)

He became acquainted with James Baillie (1737-1793), who was developing extensive plantations in Grenada and elsewhere. In 1790, Baillie bought the Bacolet and Chemin sugar estates from the Bank of England for £100,000. Samuel Mitchell was living, and perhaps working, on Baillie's Bacolet estate during that year. Very soon after purchasing the second estate, Chemin, in St George's parish in the south of Grenada, James Baillie sold it on to Samuel Mitchell, who changed its name to Hope Vale. He was now an estate owner in his own right.

At that time, Grenada was the third largest sugar producer in the British West Indies, but the terrain of St George's parish meant that a mixed economy was more productive and it is likely that the Hope Vale estate produced cocoa, coffee and cotton, as well as sugar. Grenada had a large population of free workers of mixed heritage, but Samuel Mitchell's Hope Vale was worked by at least 160 enslaved people.

Mitchell also had political and administrative responsibilities. While control of Grenada rested with a Governor, day-to-day matters were handled by the island's Council, headed by a President. Samuel Mitchell was a member of this Council and was elected President in 1790.

Over the years, Grenada had changed hands several times between Britain and France, and many of the inhabitants were francophone Catholics. In 1795 Julien Fédon (d.1796), a free planter of mixed descent, was politicised by news of the French Revolution. He led an uprising against British rule and many of Grenada's 28,000 enslaved people joined the freedom fighters. As a Colonel of the militia and member of the island Council, Samuel Mitchell would have been deeply involved. The rebels took a number of British hostages, including the Governor, Ninian Home, who was subsequently killed. An Acting Governor was appointed, but he quickly resigned. The experienced Samuel Mitchell took over the role and British army reinforcements were brought in. By the middle of 1796, Fédon's followers had been routed and the few remaining freedom fighters flung themselves off a mountain ridge rather than be captured. Colonial order was restored, but the economy of Grenada was damaged.

Fortunately for Samuel Mitchell, St George's parish in the south of the island was less affected than others further north. Nevertheless, in 1799 he returned to England to live. He retained the Hope Vale plantation and still had sufficient funds in 1799 or 1800 to purchase the Newport estate in Topsham from Thomas Floud, a local timber merchant.[56] The circumstances of Mitchell's connection with Topsham are not known, although perhaps he knew of the town through Dr Robert Hamilton of the Samaritan plantation, whose brother Sir Alexander had recently settled at *The Retreat*, which adjoined the Newport estate.

A place amongst the local elite was soon cemented. In September 1802 the *Morning Post* announced that the Hon. Samuel Mitchell, President of the Council of Grenada, was married [at St Margaret's Church, Topsham] by the Rev. James Carrington to Miss Mary Floud (1773-1861), sister to Thomas Floud, Esq. Mayor of Exeter.[57] In the register, the groom was noted as being 'of Heavitree' [in Exeter]. The new couple moved into a thatched property called *Chute's*, close to the banks of the river Exe at a place known locally as 'Newport'. Mary Elizabeth Stewart Mitchell, their first child, was born on 5 July 1803.

Less than two years later, on 4 February 1805, Samuel Mitchell suddenly died. The local newspaper paid him the following tribute:

> *On Monday last died at Newport, near Exeter, the Hon. Samuel Mitchell, president of his majesty's council at Grenada. He had spent the greatest part of his useful life in that island: where, during a period of dangerous revolt, the wisdom of his measures, and the promptitude with which they were executed, prevented it from falling into the hands of the French. For this conduct so highly honourable to his character, he received a vote of thanks from the council; and the grateful tribute of all those who were interested at this important event. In private life, he was a man whose mild virtues eminently endeared him to his family and his friends; and whose active benevolence diffused happiness through a widely extended circle.*[58]

This report confirms that within a short time, Samuel Mitchell had become a respected member of the local gentry, and that he may have used some of the money made on the plantations in Grenada on acts of charity close to home. The memorial in St Margaret's church, Topsham, records that he spent about 30 years in the West Indies, eventually becoming President of the Governing Council of Grenada and Colonel of the Colonial Militia.

Samuel's will included specific instructions for his burial:

> *I desire that my Body may be decently interred at Newport without expensive parade in the midst of the Clump of Firs on the mount overlooking the marsh*

In the Country News section of the *St James's Chronicle*, this last wish was transmitted to friends and relations in London:

> *Sunday last the remains of Samuel Mitchell, Esq. were interred pursuant to his will, in a field near his house, at Newport,*

Topsham, under a clump of trees, where a vault has been built since his decease.

The Rev. James Manning, a Dissenting Minister from Exeter, officiated.[59]

By contrast, the delayed baptism of Samuel's four-year-old daughter Mary Elizabeth Stewart Mitchell took place on 5 May 1808 in the splendid surroundings of Exeter Cathedral.

Location of Hope Vale Plantation on the Island of Grenada

Despite his sudden death, Samuel Mitchell's Hope Vale plantation in Grenada continued to operate subject to instructions left in his will and under the management of his executors and trustees:

Evan and Peter Baillie of Bristol (West India merchants, brother and nephew of Mitchell's acquaintance James Baillie), Dr John Stewart, late of Grenada (planter and British MP), Thomas Floud, of Exeter (Samuel Mitchell's father-in-law), Thomas Jarman, solicitor of Bristol.

Samuel Mitchell's personal solicitor, Mr Forbes of Ely Place, London, had recently paid off the mortgage upon Hope Vale and this suggests that the property was continuing to make a good return.

Under the terms of the will, the Hope Vale estate was to provide an annual income of £500 for Samuel's wife Mary, in addition to her life interest in the Newport estate in Topsham, and stock valued at £12,000. Samuel expressed the intention that Hope Vale be supplied with everything required to allow its staple crop, presumably sugar, to reach its full potential.

He nominated Victoire, his enslaved housekeeper at Hope Vale, and her son Frederick to be given their freedom and left gifts for them commending her *great fidelity and much attention in sickness and having conducted herself with prudence and the utmost regard to my interest particularly during the rebellion in that Island.* It is likely, but will never be known, that in the manner of many household slaves Victoire's responsibilities extended beyond mere housekeeping and that Frederick was also Samuel Mitchell's son.[60]

The business of running the plantation continued for almost 30 years under the guidance of attorneys for 'the Executors of the late Samuel Mitchell'. For some time, the attorney was Andrew Houstoun, who also managed the Samaritan Estate for Alexander Hamilton.

From 1813 and as a response to the ending of the transatlantic slave-trade, slave registers were introduced as one of a series of measures taken to improve the conditions on plantations and to ensure that numbers of enslaved workers were maintained. It can be seen that numbers on the Samaritan estate, as elsewhere, gradually fell.

On 29 October 1833, a marriage notice appeared in the local press:

> *Mary Elizabeth Stewart, only child of the late Samuel Mitchell, Esq. of Newport, Devonshire, and Vale, in the Isle of Grenada [was married] to Capt. W.J. D'Urban, of the 25th Reg. the second son of Major-General Sir Benjamin D'Urban, K.C.B. Governor of the Cape of Good Hope.[61]*

Year	Slaves	Male	Fem.	Attorney	Proprietor
1817	159	84	75		
1820	150	68	82		Executors of The late Samuel Mitchell
1821	164	80	84	Andrew Houstoun	
1823	145	78	67		
1826	148	75	73		Not known
1828	139	69	70	George Gun Monro	
1829	134	68	66		Mary Elizabeth Stewart Mitchell
1831	126	64	62	Lewis Hoyes	
1832	121	63	58		
1833	118	61	57	Thomas Cunningham	Mary E S D'Urban

Extracts from the Slave Registers for the Hope Vale Estate

The following year slavery was abolished and Mary E.S. d'Urban, Samuel Mitchell's daughter, claimed compensation for the loss of 113 enslaved people she had never met but who were working for her benefit on the Hope Vale estate. The claim was awarded in the sum of £3013 12s 7d but was contested by trustees of the financial settlement associated with her marriage. The award ended up in the hands of those trustees: John Stewart of London (the son of one of Samuel Mitchell's original executors and himself a West Indian proprietor), Samuel Trehawke Kekewich of Exminster (a local MP and sometime High Sheriff of Devon) and Samuel Parr (of Knowle House in Clyst St George, a mile from Topsham).

The enslaved people at Hope Vale would have continued to work without pay until 1838 under the apprenticeship scheme, but it is not known what eventually happened to the plantation. No buildings remain today, although there is still a village in St George's parish called Hope Vale.

In Topsham, the Mitchell and d'Urban families continued to live comfortably at Newport. Samuel Mitchell's widow Mary (1773-1861) was able to use proceeds from Samuel's business affairs in

Grenada to rebuild Newport House in 1838. Three years later, F.W.L. Ross of Broadway House in Topsham recollected that:

Near the turnpike gate is a House lately erected belonging to Mrs Mitchel called Newport; a small cottage Villa was taken down to make room for the present structure which is in the Elizabethan style.[62]

The Mitchells' two-year-old grandson William Stewart Mitchell D'Urban (1836-1934) was said to have 'assisted' in laying the foundation stone.

Mary Mitchell lived at Newport until her death in 1861 and White's Directory of 1850 describes her as one of the 'principal proprietors who have seats in the parish'.

William S.M. d'Urban, grew up to become the first curator of the Royal Albert Memorial Museum in Exeter. He in his turn lived at Newport until his death in 1934, and his daughter was living on the estate in 1939. Newport House was demolished in 1980 and subsequently became Newport Park Residential Site.

Newport House just before demolition in 1980 (Topsham Museum)

6. Sugar Plantations in Jamaica: *The Tharp Family*

Members of the Tharp family lived in Topsham from around 1834 until the end of the 19th century and had connections with several plantations in Jamaica. Linked to the Tharps by marriage were Barbara and Mary Clarke, who were independently connected to the island of Jamaica.

In 1655 Oliver Cromwell's forces captured Jamaica from Spain and 10 years later Colonel Thomas Modyford (c.1620-1679), son of an Exeter mayor, was appointed the island's new governor. He took with him 800 English planters and the brutal Slave Codes he had helped to craft in Barbados. One of these early immigrants was John Tharp.[63] The family tree of his descendants, starting in 1671 with his son John Tharp II, is shown below:

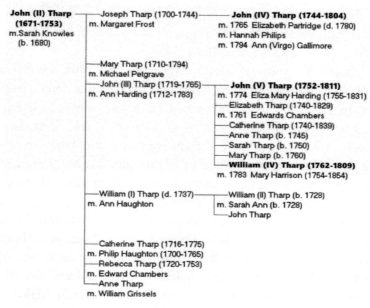

Family tree of John (II) Tharp

The Tharp family was entrepreneurial and became extremely wealthy. Chippenham Park near Cambridge, a 300-acre country estate bought by John IV Tharp in 1791, is still owned by the family and can be visited by the public.

In 1765, the brothers John V and William IV (cousins of John IV) each inherited an equal share in Green Pond, a 434-acre sugar plantation near Montego Bay. John V also acquired 798-acre Blue Hole and William IV acquired Windsor Castle, a 752-acre cattle estate. William married Mary Harrison (née Horlock) from Exeter, and it was his descendants who settled in Topsham.

Enslaved people made up three-quarters of Jamaica's population and the white elite had a constant underlying fear of rebellion. Plantation owners were expected to play their part in the military, and in 1809, when he was 47, William was killed in a riding accident:

> *At his estate, called Windsor Castle, near Montego-bay, Jamaica, William Tharp, esq. lieutenant-colonel of the St James's Regiment of Militia; who, on his return from reviewing the Regiment, on Monday the 27th of February, preceding, was thrown by a young restive horse, and conveyed speechless to his house, in which state he remained till the instant of his dissolution.*

He left four sons: John VII (aged 25), Benjamin Haughton (20), William V (16) and Thomas Reid (14).

The two older sons remained in Jamaica and took control of the estates. John managed Green Pond and owned Blue Hole. Benjamin managed Windsor Castle and owned Hampton, where he lived.

Meanwhile the two younger boys, William V and Thomas, either returned to England or were already away at school when their father was killed. They never returned to live in Jamaica, but settled instead in Devon, where a regular income from the plantations allowed them to enjoy the social lives of gentlemen.[64]

William married Mary Ventum in Bristol in 1818 and the couple set up home at Sandy Park in Drewsteignton. Four years later, this 'genteel house', with its orchard and 5.5 acres of land was offered for sale[65] and the family, now including five children, moved to St Servian in France (possibly St-Servan-sur-Mer, near St Malo), where three more children were born.

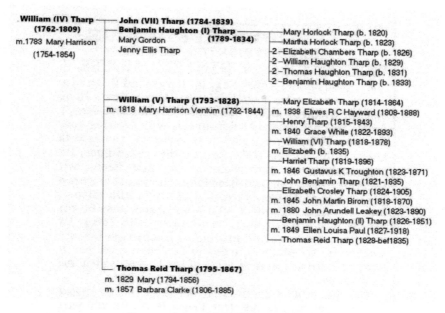

Descendants of William (IV) Tharp

Soon the youngest brother, Thomas Reid Tharp, who had been living comfortably at Seldon Cottage in Sowton, was also planning to go abroad.[66] By October 1824, Thomas and his mother Mary Tharp (née Horlock) had joined William, Mary and the children in France.[67]

They returned in July 1828 for the baptism of William and Mary's youngest son, who was christened Thomas Reid Tharp in honour of his uncle.

William was by then aged 35 and he died in Heavitree later that same year. He left his household items to his wife with the comment that he made no further provision, as on his death *she would be entitled to one-third of 'my estate in Jamaica' for life*.[68] His brothers would act as trustees and the estate would eventually pass to his children, who by then numbered eight: five boys and three girls.

The following year Thomas married a widow Mrs Mary Baird (her original family name is unknown) in St Helier, Jersey. His new wife had been born in Jamaica and was perhaps a childhood friend. It was around this time that Thomas set up home in Topsham, where members of the family were to live for a further 60 years.

Back in Jamaica, Thomas's older brothers John and Benjamin

FREEHOLD RESIDENCE,
DREWSTEIGNTON, DEVON.

TO be SOLD, a GENTEEL HOUSE, i good repair, consisting, on the ground floor, of a entrance hall, with a well staircase, two parlours 16 fee square, kitchen, dairy, and cellar; on the first floor, i front, two bed-rooms 18 feet square; with dressing-roon between 10 feet by 8, and three servants' rooms at th back, with separate staircase; on the second floor, tw bed-rooms same dimensions as the first floor, wit dressing-room. The out-door Premises consist of a brev house with room over, three-stalled stable with extensiv hay loft, a harness-room adjoining, which may be con verted into a gig-house; cow-houses with loft; tw courtlages; a large and productive kitchen garden we stocked with fruit trees, a flower garden, a small potat plat, an orchard, and 5¼ acres of land, 4 of which ma be watered.

The situation is particularly desirable to a gentlema fond of sporting, as the river Teign is within 200 yard of the premises; the country abounds with game, an no restrictions to the fair sportsman. A pack of hound are kept in the neighbourhood.

Further particulars may be known, by application t Mr. Tharp, Sandy Park, Drewsteignton.

N.B. All Letters must be post-paid.

Exeter Flying Post, *25 July 1822*

GENTEEL HOUSEHOLD FURNITURE, a Five-Year-Old PONEY; GIG and HARNESS, ONE Thorough-bred MARE, 15½ hands high, ONE Three-Year-Old FILLY, by *Beverly*, EMPTY CASKS, LARGE CORN BINN, &c. &c. property of T. Tharp, Esq: who is going abroad, for SALE, by Mr. T. Hussey, on Monday the 21st day of June inst. at Seldon Cottage, Moor-lane, two miles from Exeter.

Particulars may be had of Mr. Hedgeland, Printer, Exeter; at the place of Sale, or of the Auctioneer, Waybrook, Alphington.

Dated 9th June, 1824.   [925

Exeter Flying Post, *9 June 1824*

Haughton Tharp were still running the plantations. An extract from Ashton Warner's description of life on a sugar plantation in the 1820s highlights the differences in lifestyle between enslaved workers in the Caribbean and Tharp family members in England: [69]

> *The quantity of food allowed the slaves is from two pounds and a half to three pounds of salt-fish per week, for each grown person ... The rest of their food they raise upon their provision grounds. The owner gives to each slave from thirty to forty feet square of ground; not the best ground, but such as has been over-cropped, and is no longer productive for canes. This is taken from them the next year, when, by manuring and planting with yams and other things, it has been brought round, and recovered strength for the cultivation of sugar. ... The grounds produce plantains, yams, potatoes, pumpkins, calabashes, &c ... In building their houses, they are allowed as much board as will form a window and a door. They go to the woods and cut wild canes, to form the walls and roof. The huts are thatched with cane-trash or tops. For clothing, the owner gives to each slave in the year six yards of blue stuff, called bamboo, and six yards of brown. The young people and children are given a less allowance, in proportion to their size and age ... For bed-clothing, they give them only a blanket once in four or five years; and they are obliged to wear this till it falls in pieces.*

An earlier piece from the *Royal Gazette of Jamaica*[70] is also indicative of life on the Tharp plantations. 'Two runaways', Bob and Harry, belonging to Green Pond estate were apprehended and delivered to the St James Workhouse. (The term 'runaway' was deliberately used to suggest that escaping from bondage was a criminal act.) The Tharps would have had to pay a fee to retrieve the two men, who would undoubtedly have been harshly punished to deter others.

But times were changing and news of the possible abolition of slavery was spreading. Enslaved people who attended the Baptist chapels had been following the progress of the abolition movement and decided to strike for better working conditions. In 1832 the Baptist slave protest developed into outright rebellion. As many as 60,000 of the enslaved joined forces and took command of rural land in St James parish, where they set properties on fire. The plantation owners blamed the Baptist mission and on 8 February the militia were called out. They rode to Montego Bay and pulled down the Baptist chapel. The two Tharp brothers, Captain John Tharp and Captain Benjamin Haughton Tharp, both magistrates, were very actively engaged in the action and were later named in a report to the Baptist Missionary Society. During the struggle, known as the Baptist War, 207 freedom fighters were killed and over 300 were later executed.[71] When reports describing the brutality of the white Jamaican plantocracy reached parliament in London, the news shocked lawmakers and may have accelerated the process of emancipating the slaves. In Jamaica, the planters' view of the uprising was very different, and John Tharp later rose to the rank of Lt. Col. of the militia.

Two years later, just a few weeks before abolition of slavery became law, Benjamin Haughton Tharp decided to visit England, leaving behind his common-law wife Jenny Ellis, and a number of mixed-race children.

The *Exeter Flying Post*[72] later reported:

> *Ben. Haughton Tharp, Esq. of Jamaica, on his passage to England from that Island. Died on June 21 on board the Emma, Captain Hamilton, Master.*

By the time the will was read, slavery in the West Indies had been abolished. Benjamin Tharp bequeathed his 836-acre Hampton plantation *and the negroes and other slaves, cattle, stock and plantation utensils thereon* to his nephew and namesake Ben [Benjamin] Haughton Tharp, *youngest son*[73] of his *late dear brother William and Mary his wife*. He left £3000 currency to be shared between William's children, £2000 to his dear brother John (VII) Tharp in Jamaica, and £1500 to his brother Thomas Reid Tharp in Topsham.

An annuity on the Hampton plantation allowed payments of £100 a year to Jenny Ellis, who had been left behind in Jamaica, for the support and education of his [Benjamin's] natural children with her, and thereafter £25 a year for herself. A further £2000 was left in trust for his reputed children (Elizabeth Chambers Tharp, Thomas Haughton Tharp, William Haughton Tharp and Benjamin Haughton

Tharp) and £100 each in cash to two other reputed children (Mary Horlock Tharp and Martha Horlock Tharp), possibly the children of a previous relationship with Mary Gordon. The further history of these six Tharp children of mixed descent is unknown.

At the time of abolition in 1834, the white members of the Tharp family consisted of the matriarch Mary (William IV's widow, now 80 years old), her eldest son John VII (still in Jamaica), her son William V's widow and her children, and her youngest son Thomas. Their 'assets' are recorded as:

> *Green Pond Estate, St James, Jamaica: 104 slaves, 36 stock*
> *Hampton Estate, St James, Jamaica: 125 slaves, 21 stock*
> *Windsor Castle, St. James, Jamaica: 93 slaves, 45 stock*
> *Blue Hole, Hanover, Jamaica: 119 slaves, 25 stock*

The listing together of enslaved people and animal stock (cattle) within official records and newspaper reporting is typical for the time, deliberately dehumanising the enslaved in order to legitimise slavery itself.

In 1834, in compensation for the loss of these 447 enslaved workers, the British government paid monetary awards to the Tharp family:

Claimant	Estate	Award
John VII	Windsor Castle (2 shares)	£1304 1s 9d
John VII	Green Pond	£2076 0s 2d
John VII	Blue Hole	£2264 7s 7d
Mary, William V's widow	Windsor Castle	£186 6s 6d
Ben H Tharp (William V's 8-year-old son)	Hampton	£2397 2s 7d
Thomas (in trust for William V's children)		£1304 1s 9d

Compensation paid to members of Tharp family

John VII died at Green Pond in 1839 and administration of his estate passed to his brother Thomas in Topsham.

After emancipation, the Tharps continued to live comfortably in Topsham, while maintaining links with other families in Jamaica.

Thomas did not receive compensation on his own account, he seems never to have had a profession and yet lived the comfortable life of a gentleman. In the censuses of 1841 and 1851 he is listed in Seabrook House, near the gate on the Topsham-Exeter turnpike, with his wife Mary, his mother Mary Tharp (née Horlock) and a servant. Just across the road, Mary Mitchell settled into Newport House, her recently rebuilt, Elizabethan-style home.

On the night of the 1851 census, Thomas's wife Mary was paying a visit to her unmarried friend, Barbara Clarke (1806-1885), who lived just a mile away at Barton Cottage in Topsham High Street. Barbara was listed as a 'landed proprietor' who, like Mary and Thomas Tharp, had been born in Jamaica. She was the younger daughter of John and Mary Clarke and had been born on their Weymouth plantation in the parish of St Ann's. Her parents died young, and Barbara and her sister Mary West Clarke (1803-1890) returned to England as small children to live with their uncle James Clarke. Their new home was initially in Exeter, but by 1822 they had moved to Strand, Topsham. The Weymouth estate in Jamaica was administered by another uncle William Clarke who was relied on to *remit annually ... a sufficiency from the produce of their* [Mary and Barbara's] *late father's estate.*[74] On emancipation in 1834, William Clarke applied for compensation on behalf of his brother's estate and was awarded £1132 2s 10d for the loss of 51 enslaved people. This award benefited the two Clarke girls, who also enjoyed Weymouth estate profits until at least 1838,

Miniature of Barbara Clarke

at which time 39 apprentices (newly-free people) were employed.

At a time just before the invention of photography, a miniature was produced of 25-year-old Barbara, painted on ivory and inscribed on the reverse, *15 June 1831, Topsham.* In 2018, it appeared at an Exeter auction house.[75]

The following decade saw the deaths of the two Mary Tharps and their burials in Topsham Cemetery: *Mary, relict of William Tharp of Windsor Castle, Jamaica, who departed this life on the 23rd Dec 1854, aged 100,*[76] and *on 20 March 1856 at Sea Brook Cottage died Mary, the beloved wife of T.R. Tharp.*[77]

Thomas did not remain a widower for long. In the summer of 1857, he married Barbara Clarke at St Margaret's church and the couple appeared on the 1861 census living in Barbara's house, Barton Cottage, on the corner of High Street and Pound Lane (now Denver Road). Barton Cottage is a two-storey brick and Heavitree stone house and Thomas and Barbara kept two live-in servants.

Thomas Reid Tharp predeceased Barbara and when she died, in 1885, she left an estate of £8768 8s 9d. On 3 December 1885, the *Western Times* advertised the sale of the contents of Barton Cottage, Barbara's Topsham property, providing an indication of her comfortable lifestyle.

Auctions

AUCTION THIS DAY
BARTON COTTAGE, TOPSHAM.
(Residence of Mrs B Tharp, deceased).

SECOND DAY, (Dec 3rd).—The Furniture in Dining Room, Table Lamps, Chimney Ornaments, richly cut Table Glass, Bed and Table Linen, Musical Box, handsome Electro Plate, China Dinner and Dessert Sets, Water Color Drawings, &c.

THIRD DAY, (Dec 4).—The Contents of Entrance Hall, Drawing Room, and Kitchens, Cottage Pianoforte, Musical Box, valuable English and Foreign China, old line and Mezzotinto India proof Engravings, Water Color Drawings, 200 Vols. of Books, Curious and Antique Art Needlework Bed Furniture, Crown Derby Dinner and Dessert Sets, Nankin China, Wines and Spirits, Plants in pots, &c.

Catalogues (3d each) at the House, or of the AUCTIONEERS, Queen Street Road, Exeter.

Sale each day at Eleven.

Delivery one hour after the day's sale is closed.

BEST and COMMIN, Auct'oneers.

Western Times, *3 December 1885*

The last of the Tharps known to have lived in Topsham were the sons and daughters of Thomas's brother, William V, who had died soon after he returned from France in 1828:

Mary (born 1814)	John (born 1821)
Henry (born 1815)	Elizabeth (born 1824)
William VI (born 1818)	Benjamin Haughton (born 1826)
Harriet (born 1819)	Thomas Reid (born 1828)

Two of the five sons died young: Thomas Reid II was under seven; John died when he was 14 and was buried in St Margaret's churchyard on 27 December 1835. His death was announced in the local newspaper.[78]

In 1838 the eldest of the daughters, Mary (1814-1864), married E.R.C(harles) Hayward (1806-1888) a fundholder and annuitant. Mary died when she was 50 years old, and two years later Charles married Mary West Clarke (1803-1890), the sister of Barbara Tharp (née Clarke) of Barton Cottage and joint heiress to the Weymouth plantation in Jamaica. Mary West Clarke's life between 1823, when she lived with her aunt and uncle in Strand and 1864 when she married, is unknown, but she clearly retained strong links with Topsham. The wedding took place at St Margaret's church and the couple set up home at Mount Howe Villa.[79] Later that same year, Charles's daughter from his first marriage to Mary Tharp, died and was buried in Topsham cemetery. Her orphaned three-year-old son Edward Dwight grew up with Charles and Mary West Hayward (née Clarke) at Mount Howe Villa. Edward would have derived benefit from slave labour on the Tharp's Windsor Castle plantation through his deceased grandmother's estate and the Clarke's Weymouth plantation through his step-grandmother.

William V's second daughter was Harriet (1819-1896). In 1846 she married Gustavus Kempenfeldt Troughton (1826-1871), a 23-year-old fund-holder and annuitant. A year earlier, the youngest daughter Elizabeth (1824-1905) had married John M. Birom (1821-1871),[80] a local doctor who had been baptised in Topsham in 1821. Elizabeth and John may have been related – he was the godson (and possibly also the illegitimate son) of Elizabeth's great-uncle, John Horlock. Coincidentally, the husbands of these two sisters died within months of each other and the 1871 census shows Harriet and Elizabeth living together at The Dutch House, Strand with their maternal aunt.[81] After the aunt died (buried in Topsham in 1875),[82] Harriet moved away and by 1881 was living in Kensington, London. Elizabeth re-married at St Margaret's church, describing her late father William V's occupation as an Officer in the Surrey militia. Her new husband was Rev. John Arundell Leakey (1823-1890), vicar of Topsham, whose wife had recently died. Elizabeth became stepmother to a large family and moved with them to a new parish at Gerrans in Cornwall.

Two more of the sons, Henry (1815-1843) and William (1818-1878), are remembered together at Topsham cemetery. In 1878, the *Exeter and Plymouth Gazette* carried the news that there had died *on November 4, at Topsham, William Tharp VI Esq., last surviving son of the late W. Tharp V, Esq., St James's, Jamaica, aged 60.*[83] His widow Elizabeth remained at Sea View Cottage, 46 Strand. William's grave carries an inscription commemorating his older brother Henry, *who died in Jamaica in 1843, aged 28 and his wife Grace, born 1822, died 1893.* After Henry's death, Grace returned from Jamaica and in 1891 was living at Shell House, Strand.

Memorial inscription to Henry Tharp and his wife Grace, Topsham cemetery

The last of the eight children, and the youngest boy to achieve adulthood, was Ben Haughton Tharp II, who inherited the Hampton plantation from his uncle Benjamin Haughton Tharp (I). As an eight-year-old slave owner, he had received £2397 2s 7d in compensation from the government. Like his older brother Henry, he emigrated to Jamaica as an adult, but came back to marry Ellen Louisa Paul (1827-1918) of Strand, Topsham at St Margaret's church in 1849.[84]

The couple returned to Ben's inherited estate but an inscription in Jamaica[85] records what happened next:

> BEN HAUGHTON THARP, of Hampton, St James, Esq., Justice of the Peace, d. 24 July 1851 aged 25
> THOMAS REID THARP, only child of Ben Haughton and Ellen Louisa Tharp, d. 3 Sept. 1851 aged 15 months

Ben Tharp's death was explained in the *Hampshire Chronicle*:[86]

> July 24 at Jamaica, by a fall from his horse, which had taken fright during a severe thunder storm, Ben H Tharp Esq. of Hampton one of the H M Justices of the Peace for that Island. He was held in high estimation by all classes and will be long and deservedly lamented, aged 25. Youngest son of the late William Tharp Esq.

The accident leading to his death paralleled that which befell his grandfather William Tharp IV in 1809, who perished having been *thrown by a young restive horse*. Ellen Tharp returned to England and settled in Richmond, Surrey. Amongst her effects when she died in 1918 were shares in the Great Western Railway, perhaps purchased with some of the compensation money Ben Tharp received as a child. It illustrates in a small way how the proceeds of slavery contributed to much of the infrastructure of Britain today.

The Tharp family were pillars of the community. In 1887, St Margaret's Church was reconsecrated after renovation work. Following the service, a luncheon was held in the schoolroom, presided over by Sir J.T.B. Duckworth of Newcourt House. Amongst the guests were Mrs T.R. (Barbara) Tharp, Mrs (Harriet) Troughton, Mr C.E. (Charles) Hayward, Mrs (Elizabeth) Leakey and Mrs (Elizabeth) Tharp. Barbara Tharp also placed money in trust for the community, and this fund is still drawn upon for local charitable purposes.

It is worth at this point mentioning the Tharp's servants in Topsham. The interconnected Harris and Tancock families worked for various members of the Tharp family in Topsham from before 1840 until at least 1881, when 15-year-old Harriet Tancock was living and working as a general servant for Elizabeth Tharp at 46 Strand. While they probably knew little of Tharp family history and nothing of plantation life, their wages were ultimately derived from the unpaid labour of enslaved people thousands of miles away. In this insidious way, plantation profits and compensation monies found their way into communities throughout Britain and its empire.

All these Tharp family members lived comfortable lives in Topsham, owning or leasing houses, employing servants and taking part in the social life of the town as 'gentlemen' or 'annuitants'. Their respectable, privileged lives were supported by money earned from slave labour. While much is known of the Tharps' lives in Topsham, very little can be told of what happened to Hampton, Green Pond, Windsor Castle or Blue Hole, the plantations that belonged to the family in Jamaica. Of the generations of enslaved people who lived, toiled and died there, nothing is known at all.

7. Topsham in Jamaica: *The Davy Family*

James Davy (1729-1813) was a tenant farmer who moved from Heavitree in Exeter to Countess Wear in 1766. He farmed Wear Barton Farm and was a lime and coal merchant, building lime kilns and a quay in 1780. He married Mary Carter in 1758 and the couple produced eight children, Rebecca, Joan, Robert, James, John, Mary, Thomas and Edward. Seven of these eight children can be directly or indirectly connected to the enslavement of people in Jamaica.

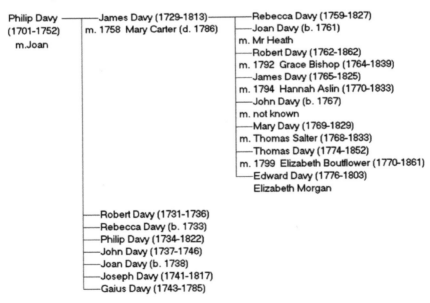

The Davy family of Wear, Topsham

Robert Davy (1762-1862), the eldest son and most celebrated family member, took over his father's business and branched out into ship-building, first of his own limestone-carrying boats and later as a constructor of large sailing ships. He purchased the Passage shipyard in Topsham and became a major local employer and a shipbuilder of national importance. He never owned a slave, nor had a financial interest in a plantation, but his businesses supported slavery and he gained financially from its continuation.

At the time of the Davy shipyard, the most important responsibility of the Royal Navy after the defence of Britain, was patrolling the sea lanes. Robert Davy became a government contractor, supplying Naval gunships. Some of the vessels built in the Topsham yards were used to defend Britain's valuable colonial possessions in America and the Caribbean.

Davy also built commercial ships including West Indiamen – the cargo vessels designed to trade with the Caribbean islands – and some of these ships may have been crewed by men from Topsham.

The 228-ton West Indiaman *Grace* was named after Robert's wife and was launched in 1799. The *Exeter Flying Post* ran an advert:

> *For Kingston, Jamaica, now lying at Topsham, the good ship Grace ... being just launched. Is neatly fitted up for the convenience of passengers, will sail the next convoy in March ... N.B. A respectable person is going out in the above vessel to settle at Jamaica, and will be glad to transact business on the usual terms.*[87]

The identity of the 'respectable person' is not known.

Davy part-owned *Grace* until 1801. Nine years later, he built a larger ship, *Jamaica Planter*.[88] It was sold to London merchants but again Robert retained part ownership and the ship sailed to Jamaica, returning with sugar, rum, coffee and pimento (a spice extracted from berries), the products of slave labour. *Jamaica Planter* met an untimely end on its second voyage, when it became separated from its convoy in rough seas near Bermuda and disappeared without trace.

A year after building *Jamaica Planter*, Robert Davy had better luck when he built *Medina*, a 500-ton merchant ship.[89] He retained a financial interest in this ship until October 1821, during which time

Medina made 10 annual voyages to Jamaica, sailing in late autumn and returning in July. This fits the usual pattern of loading sugar in Jamaica in spring and sailing for England before the start of the summer hurricane season. Amongst further West Indiamen built in the Davy shipyard were *Earl St Vincent* and *Mary*, perhaps named after his mother or sister.

Medina, *Churchman's cigarette card, issued 1936 (Topsham Museum)*

Robert Davy had a long and successful life, living to within a few weeks of his 100th birthday. He became a very wealthy man and was a leader in the development of Topsham. He was also seen as a great supporter of the poor, but some of the money came from trade with the plantations. He built a substantial house in Mill Road, Countess Wear (now called Waring Bowen House) and is remembered for widening the bridge at Countess Wear and substantially funding the construction of Topsham Lock. On the outskirts of Topsham, Robert Davy Road was recently named to celebrate his memory.

Of the other children of James and Mary Davy, three chose to keep close to home. The eldest Rebecca (1759-1827) did not marry and appears to have stayed at home with her parents. Mary (1769-1829) married a yeoman farmer, Thomas Salter, in Topsham in 1789 and is the only child who has no apparent links with slavery. Thomas (1774-1852) trained as a doctor and settled in Ottery St Mary, 10 miles to the east.

The rest of the family sought their fortunes in Jamaica.[90][91] They left England around 1790, at a time when some liberal thinkers were beginning to question the morality of slavery and the tide of public opinion was just beginning to turn.

James (b.1765), John (b.1767), and Edward (b.1776) turned to farming. At the time the Davy siblings emigrated, the main economic activity in Jamaica was sugar cultivation. The cutting and processing was done by enslaved labour, but the heavy work of hauling cane carts from the fields to the sugar factories and of turning the machinery to grind the cane was often done by oxen. James and John, and to a lesser extent younger Edward, had no doubt learned a lot about cattle during their childhood on Wear Barton Farm. The brothers bought land in Manchester parish, in the mountainous centre of Jamaica, where it was too cool, too steep and too dry for sugar, but ideal for cattle. They set about raising the sturdy animals essential to the sugar plantations on the coastal plains and planted additional land with coffee and pimento.

Workers were needed to look after their cattle and tend the crops and the brothers would have been able to visit the slave-auction in Montego Bay or at the harbour run by the Tharp family on the Martha Brae River. The adverts below are from *The Royal Gazette of Jamaica*, 1794:

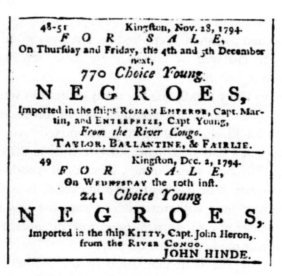

Royal Gazette of Jamaica, *6 December 1794*

Transcriptions of the *Jamaica Almanacs*[92] show that the properties purchased by the Davy brothers were called 'Topsham' and 'Wear Pen', reflecting the localities where they had grown up.[93] However, it appears that they were not the first to occupy or name these areas. A map of 1764[94] shows them owned by John Griffith and John King respectively. Nothing is known of these previous owners, nor of their possible connections to Topsham and Countess Wear. Perhaps they had historical connections with the Davy family and the brothers set out intending to take over these particular plantations, or perhaps they were drawn to the Manchester area because of the attraction of these familiar place names.

48   Kingston, Nov. 29, 1794.
RAN AWAY, on Thursday the 6th inst. a negro man named TOPSHAM, a Mundingo, about six feet high, walks remarkably upright, and has a very good head of hair; formerly belonged to Thomas Gray, Esq. deceased. Whoever apprehends said negro, and lodges him in the workhouse, or brings him to the subscriber, shall receive a Guinea reward.
                                    R. HENDERSON.

Royal Gazette of Jamaica, *29 November 1794*

A fugitive named Topsham, reported as a runaway[95] in 1794, may once have been enslaved by one of these men who had emigrated from Topsham in Devon.[96]

Transferred to Davy hands, the Topsham plantation was first owned by Edward (1776-1803), the youngest of the brothers. He had a relationship with Elizabeth Morgan, a free mixed-race woman, and together they had a daughter, Jane. Edward died in 1803, at the age of 27. He left Elizabeth some money, 25 acres of woodland and *three negro women* – that is, he left her three domestic slaves. He left £1000 to their daughter Jane with instructions that she was *to be sent to England at the age of eight years to have a decent education*. It is not known if she ever made the journey.

Edward left the Topsham plantation to his brother Thomas and sister Rebecca, who were still in Devon. They became absentee landlords, never visiting the Topsham estate, nor taking any active part in its operation. Nevertheless, the property was run for their benefit and from 1803 onwards they profited from the labour of enslaved people. When Rebecca died in 1827, she left her share of the property to Thomas.[97]

James Davy settled at Wear Pen (the name 'pen' means cattle farm) in Jamaica, just north of the Topsham plantation. He married Hannah Aslin in St Elizabeth, Jamaica in 1794 and around 1800, he built Wear Pen house for his new family.

Wear Pen House. Manchester, Jamaica in 2007 [photo James Glanville]

Three children were born during the second half of the 1790s: Mary Elizabeth, Anne Maria and James Lewis. All three were baptised on the same day in 1800 in St Elizabeth parish and registered as white, indicating that Hannah was also white. The couple subsequently had four more children in the early 1800s: John was baptised in Exminster in 1801, George in Topsham in 1803, and Frances and Eliza were baptised together in Alphington in 1808.[98]

James was clearly doing well as he could afford to bring his family from Jamaica to Devon for all these occasions. He came home at least once more – his father's will was written in February 1813 and mentions that James (he describes him as a 'merchant') was 'now on passage to Jamaica'. By 1810, James Davy is recorded as being the owner of 'Wear', with 75 slaves and 256 livestock.

The people enslaved on the Davy estates seem to have fared better than many of their contemporaries, with numbers remaining steady or even increasing slowly:

> *The whole rationale behind the slave trade was that, as 'slaves' were property and could therefore be regarded solely as economic entities, it made business sense to work them hard – so hard that women's health did not allow them to have many children. The death rate was higher than the birth rate in nearly all parts of the West Indies except for the coffee-growing regions. The explanation may lie in the high altitude [of the coffee plantations], above the level of many tropical diseases, and the less arduous nature of the work. These people were not working in gangs in the cane fields under close supervision all day, as was the lot of most of those enslaved on the plantations.*[99]

Year	Slaves	Stock	Attorney	Proprietor	Plantation
1810	75	256		James Davy	Wear
1812	76	249		James Davy	Wear
1816	82	302		James Davy	Wear
1817	85	323		James Davy	Wear
1818	86	326		James Davy	Wear
1820	95	341		James Davy	Wear
1821	92	382		James Davy	Wear
1822	91	399		James Davy	Wear
1823	90	365	John Davy	James Davy	Wear
1824	92	395		James Davy	Wear
1825	92	430		James Davy	Wear
1826	96	359	John Coley	James L Davy	Wear
1827	94	334		James L Davy	Wear

Enslaved persons and stock at James Davy's Wear Plantation

In his public life, James was a pillar of the white community. The *Jamaica Almanacs* Civil Lists record him under *Assistant Judges and Magistrates* in 1802 and 1824, when he would have made judgements concerning the lives of enslaved people. He was a Captain in the militia (similar to the territorial army) and donated land for the building of St George's Anglican Church which served the white elite. This church has fallen into disrepair, but until recently it contained marble plaques and tombstones in memory of the Davy family.

Although James Davy died in Jamaica, the family tomb in Clyst St Mary churchyard bears the inscription, '*To the memory of James Davy Esquire, late of the Island of Jamaica, who died October 19th, 1825, aged 60*'.

Originally, James had nominated his brothers Robert (of Topsham) and Thomas (of Ottery St Mary) as his executors, but a later codicil to the will substituted his sons James Lewis and John, together with a friend and fellow planter, John Coley.

The 1826 Slave Register[100] refers to the enslaved people 'in possession' of John Coley (as Executor to James Davy deceased) in the parish of Manchester, Jamaica. The Register required managers to account for the increases and decreases in numbers and their causes. In the column headed 'Increase or cause thereof', it was acceptable to enter 'By death', with no further explanation, and the ages of the slaves when they died are indicative of the hard lives they led.

Extract from the 1826 slave register for Manchester

The first on the list is called 'Topsham'. This would not have been his birth name. It was common practice for slaveholders to name or re-name enslaved people on a whim. The formerly enslaved Olaudah Equiano recalled:

> *In this place I was called Jacob, but on board the African snow* [a two-masted ship] *I was called Michael. While I was on board* [a ship bound for England] *my captain and master named me Gustavus Vassa.*

To have one's name taken away when home, traditions and freedom have also been lost is particularly cruel.

In the years leading up to emancipation, baptism of enslaved people was encouraged as it strengthened the argument for emancipation. A newly-baptised person received a Christian name and a surname, and when 103 people enslaved on Wear Pen were baptised on 10 March 1820, most chose the surname 'Davy'.[101]

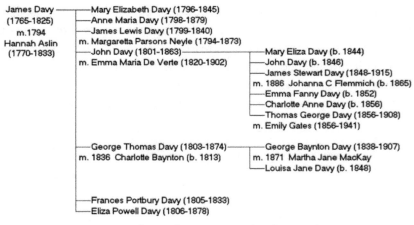

Descendants of James Davy (1765-1825)

Year	Slaves	Stock	Proprietor	Plantation
1812	33	3	Edward Davy (executors)	Topsham
1816	38	6	Thomas & Rebecca Davy	Topsham
1817	39	9	Thomas & Rebecca Davy	Topsham
1818	40	7	Thomas & Rebecca Davy	Topsham
1820	39	9	Thomas & Rebecca Davy	Topsham
1821	39	8	Thomas & Rebecca Davy	Topsham
1822	43	8	Thomas & Rebecca Davy	Topsham
1823	43	8	Thomas & Rebecca Davy	Topsham
1824	47	6	Thomas & Rebecca Davy	Topsham
1825	12		John Davy	Dunsinane
	48	15	John Davy	Robin's Hall
1826	50	16	John Davy	Robin's Hall
1827	6	10	John Davy	Robin's Hall

Enslaved persons and stock at the Davy Topsham Plantation and other estates owned or managed by John Davy

General view of Topsham, Jamaica (James Glanville 2007)

Topsham Church, (James Glanville, 2007)

Of the second generation of the Davy family in Jamaica, it was James's son John (1801-1863) who was eventually left as the manager of their property on the island. He may be found listed in the *Jamaica Almanacs* as manager of an increasingly large portfolio of properties during the final years of slavery.

He had taken over management of Wear Pen in 1824 when James became ill and perhaps returned to England. Following his father's example, John Davy served as a Magistrate or Assistant Judge at the courthouse near Wear Pen in 1824, 1839 and 1851, and rose through the ranks to become a Major in the Manchester Militia Regiment of Foot.

Property	1828	1829	1831	1832	1833
Allsides					29
Asia					51
Berry Hill					203
Bombay	27	27			
Green Hill			27	27	27
Green Pond			180	144	150
Green Vale			87	100	99
Hanbury & Russell Place	39	39	220		
	129	133			
Knowsley Park		*7	55	54	57
Litchfield	65		69	72	70
Parke Hall					97
Robin's Hall	50	49	46	28	
Vauxhall	18	18			
Vere Parish					40
Wear Pen	95	**95	97	102	101

Properties owned or managed by John Davy and number of people enslaved [102]

One of the properties managed by John Davy was Topsham, owned by his aunt and uncle Rebecca and Thomas Davy, who lived back home in Devon. When Rebecca died in 1827, she had left her share of Topsham to her brother Thomas, and he initially seems to have planned the sale of the estate but later changed his mind.[103]

7–10   Mile-Gully, Feb. 7, 1828.

FOR SALE, TOPSHAM Plantation, in Mile-Gully, consisting of 275 Acres, 40 Acres of which are in Coffee, 90 Acres in Guinea-Grass, partially fenced, and the remainder in ruinate Coffee, Provision-Grounds, Woodland, &c.

ALSO,

HOG-HOLE, consisting of 300 Acres of Land, fit for the cultivation of Coffee, adjoining Chudleigh, the Farm, and Knowsley-Park Plantations.

JOHN DAVY.

Royal Gazette of Jamaica, *23 February 1828*

When slavery was abolished, John and his brother James Lewis Davy applied for compensation as slave owners losing their 'property'. They were awarded £2156 11s 1d for the 106 people freed from Wear. The Davy brothers were now cash rich.

James Lewis Davy, who like his brother Thomas had become a medical doctor, briefly returned to England in 1834 to marry Margaretta Abell in Tormoham, near Torquay. Margaretta's husband, William, had died on passage to England in 1832, when he was described by the *Exeter Flying Post* as *for many years a respectable planter in Jamaica*. In 1839, James was appointed *Custos Rotulorum*,[104] the chief magistrate of Manchester Parish, but the following year he died, aged 42.

In 1841 when he was 40 years old, John also visited England to marry. He chose English-born Emma Maria D'Everlé, who was almost 20 years his junior. They went on to have six children Mary, John, James, Emma and twins Charlotte and Thomas, all born at Wear Pen in Jamaica.

At least two plantations were managed by John Davy on behalf of his uncle Dr Thomas Davy in Ottery St Mary. In 1833, Thomas was awarded £1101 3s 8d for the loss of labour by 59 enslaved people. He bought the best house in Ottery St Mary (The Raleigh House) and was able to provide a good education for his three sons who became a doctor, a solicitor and an inventor.

After emancipation, the economy of Jamaica went into decline as the planters found it increasingly difficult to make a profit when they had to pay their workforce. John appears to have prospered at first and he acquired Heavy Tree, an estate in the mountain north of Wear, apparently recalling his father's Heavitree roots.[105] By 1845 the economic crisis was causing many owners to default on their mortgages or abandon their properties altogether. Both Wear and Heavy Tree (a combined total of 2167 acres) were in receivership by the late 1850s and John Davy and his family returned to Britain, supposedly bankrupt.

Davy plaque in St George's church, Wear Pen (Geoffrey Davy 2011)

They set up home with three female servants at 26 Royal Crescent, Kensington and John Davy died there in 1863. Two of his sons, James and Thomas, went to Uppingham School and Oxford University. Thomas became a doctor and went to Australia to live. Mary Eliza, the eldest daughter, eventually returned to Jamaica, where she died in 1911.

As a footnote to the Davy plantations in Jamaica, an episode of the BBC's *Who Do You Think You Are* followed the family history of TV chef Ainsley Harriott. His ancestor Joan Davy was a slave at Wear Pen and in 1831 aged 15 she had a daughter Catherine fathered by the overseer Jonathan Briggs. For plantation owners it made good economic sense to keep the slave stock high, and sexual exploitation was positively encouraged throughout the colonies. Joan was finally granted freedom when Catherine was seven.

Other people living in Jamaica today have the family name Davy and may be descendants of the enslaved people who worked the Davy plantations. There is still a village called Davyton in Manchester Parish and Hubert Davy, a mixed-race man of the Windrush generation, came to London in the 1950s from the Wear Pen area where his family had farmed for generations.[106]

8. Virginia, Jamaica and Topsham:
The Goodrich Family

While sugar was the premier crop in the Caribbean, in Virginia it was tobacco. Like sugar, tobacco was fashionable, addictive and required large numbers of workers to pick and process the crop. The first Africans were trafficked in 1619 and in 1662 Virginia passed a law to make slavery hereditary:

All children born in this county shall be held, bond or free, according to the condition of their mother.

A second law was passed a few years later. It set the conditions for managing the slaves:

If any slave shall resist their master, mistress or overseer they may be corrected. If by the extremity of the correction [a slave] should chance to die, his death shall not be a felony.

Olaudah Equiano was taken to Virginia around 1755 as a child slave. He later recalled:

I had seen a black woman slave as I came through the house, who was cooking the dinner, and the poor creature was cruelly loaded with various kinds of iron machines; she had one particularly on her head, which locked her mouth so fast she could scarcely speak; and could not eat or drink. I was much astonished and shocked by this contrivance, which I afterwards learned was called the iron muzzle. Soon after I had a fan put into my hand, to fan the gentleman while he slept.[107]

Enslaved Africans were considered as property to be bought, sold and bred like cattle. They were often expected to work from dawn to dusk with limited food, clothing and medical attention. They were not allowed to learn how to read or write and at any moment parents, siblings and children could be sold. By the 18th century, nearly all wealth in Virginia was derived from investments in slavery and all businesses and exports were touched by it.

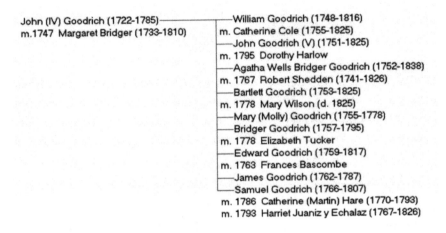

Children of John Goodrich and Margaret Bridger

One of the most notorious of Topsham's slave-owning residents came from a South Virginia family of tobacco planters whose immigrant ancestor had patented land there in 1654.[108]

John Goodrich was born in 1722 and he and his sons were legends in their day. John married Margaret Bridger, the daughter of another prosperous local family, and together they had two daughters and seven sons.

During the first dozen years of his marriage, John Goodrich added nearly 1500 acres to the family tobacco estate in Nansemond County and 450 acres in neighbouring Isle of Wight County. He developed a merchant shipping business and by 1774 had a fleet of 12 merchant vessels, mainly small sloops and schooners.[109] He also possessed wharves, dry goods stores and warehouses. The company operated mainly out of Portsmouth, Virginia and the fleet traded agricultural and timber commodities to the West Indies and to other ports in the colonies. Some of Goodrich's enslaved workers were pilots and tradesmen and his sons were trained to take over the business as 'planter-shippers'.

In 1767 Robert Shedden, a Scottish emigré from Ayrshire, married John Goodrich's 15-year-old daughter Agatha, and became his father-in-law's business partner.[110]

After years of increasing tension between Britain and the settlers, the American War of Independence began in 1775. The hostilities threatened merchants like Goodrich, with blockades cutting off imports and exports, and privateers from both sides attacking merchant vessels.

John Goodrich was motivated more by profit than politics. When fighting broke out, the Royal Governor of Virginia, Lord Dunmore, seized the colony's supply of gunpowder from the arsenal in Williamsburg. The Goodrich family contracted to assist the Patriot cause by collecting £5000-worth of gunpowder from the West Indies and bringing it back without attracting notice of the crown authorities.[111]

The mission proved to be a disaster. Although the gunpowder reached its destination, an intercepted letter from Robert Shedden to his father-in-law John Goodrich exposed the conspiracy to Lord Dunmore and he arrested Shedden and one of Goodrich's sons. John Goodrich was forced to do a deal. He switched sides and aligned himself with Lord Dunmore and the Loyalist cause.

Dunmore reported on the Goodrich family in a letter:[112]

> *The male part consists of a Father and seven Sons, five of whom are arrived to the age of manhood, who are now most zealously engaged in His Majesty's Service. Four of them are perfectly well acquainted with every River, Creek, or Branch within this bay. I have now five of their Vessels employed constantly running up the Rivers, where they have orders to seize, burn or destroy everything that is water born … They have all left their Houses, Negroes, Plantations, Stocks, and everything else at the Mercy of the Rebels, and are now with their whole Family Water Born in this Fleet.*

Goodrich's career as a Loyalist did not start well. The Patriots, confused about his intentions and owed money from the gunpowder deal, sequestered his lands and property. When one of his sons was caught trying to move *slaves and stock* from the seized property, the enslaved people were *secured* and the stock put up for auction. Valuable molasses and salt were confiscated from the Goodrich warehouses in Portsmouth and his house and two of his ships were burned as a warning to others not to work with Lord Dunmore.

Under his agreement with Dunmore, two of Goodrich's remaining ships were commissioned into government service and operated as privateers, capturing American navy and trading ships and confiscating their cargoes. It was a risky business. Patriots captured Goodrich in North Carolina on 17 April 1776 and by May he was in a Virginia jail. Found guilty of treason, his entire estate was confiscated and he was kept under guard, effectively a prisoner of war. Somehow, John Goodrich escaped and the family moved to New York, which was still under loyalist control. Their privateering operation grew to four fighting vessels; the largest, *Dunmore*, was a sixteen-gun ship.[113] John Goodrich and his sons were among the most notorious of the Loyalist privateers and their prize money made it an extremely lucrative business.

Meanwhile, Robert Shedden was obliged to flee with Agatha and their family in company with Lord Dunmore's fleet and his property in Virginia was confiscated. He took refuge in Bermuda in 1776, and afterwards in New York. When peace was declared in 1783, he returned to England and established a successful mercantile business with his sons, trading in tobacco, sugar and rum.

John Goodrich also left the United States and settled in England, having lost both land and an unknown number of enslaved people. He settled in Topsham with his wife Margaret and their two youngest sons, James and Samuel, where they were supported by a small Government pension and contributions from older sons who had achieved financial independence.

John did not live long to enjoy his new life. He died in November 1785, aged 63 years, and was interred at Topsham Church. The stone marking his burial place within St Margaret's was obscured beneath pews during the re-building of the church in 1874 and 1877, but fortunately the inscription was noted and recorded.[114] It reads:

Beneath this tomb are deposited the remains of John Goodrich, Esq., who died the 17th November 1785, and left behind him a widow, seven sons and one daughter, being 63 years old. He was a native of Virginia and generously submitted to the depredation of an ample fortune in supporting his loyalty at the commence-ment of the American Rebellion.

John and Margaret Goodrich's son James died two years later, aged just 23, and was also interred at Topsham. A memorial to him and later members of the family is located within the church tower on the west wall.

The widowed Margaret Goodrich seems to have been retained by her family in some comfort and an indication of the house in which she and her son Samuel initially lived in Topsham is given in an extract from a contemporary deed:[115]

> In the Vault under the Family Seat opposite this Monument, are deposited the Remains of JOHN GOODRICH Esq a Native of *Virginia* in *North America* who departed this Life in November 1785, aged 63 Years. And of MARGARET his Wife, who died 12 April 1810, aged 78 Years. Also of Two of their Sons, JAMES GOODRICH, who died 26 May 1787, aged 23 Years; And SAMUEL GOODRICH, who died 26 October 1807, aged 41 Years. Also JAMES GOODRICH, Son of SAMUEL GOODRICH, who died 8 November 1836, aged 47 Years. And SARAH GOODRICH, his Wife who died 20 April 1854, Aged 65 Years.

Memorial in Church Tower

> *David Sweetland, his mortgagor and Trustee to Daniel Follet – Names: Milford and Clark, Benjamin Follett. Messuage or tenement situated on the Strand near the building place, heretofore built on part of a field, Lower Lime Kiln Field, in possession of James Macy, afterwards of James Jackson, since of ...... Hill, spinster, late of Sarah Ouchterloney, now of* **Margaret Goodrich**.

During the following decade, Margaret Goodrich moved to a house in Monmouth Street, Topsham, which was offered for sale in 1806:[116]

> *To be sold by private contract for the residue of a term of 4000 years, a neat and convenient DWELLING-HOUSE, and*

*walled garden, in the occupation of **Mrs. Goodrich**, situate at the higher end of Monmouth-street; ... an auction will be held at the Globe Tavern, Exeter, on Wednesday the tenth day of September next, at four o'clock in the afternoon ... August 26, 1806.*

Following the sale, Margaret Goodrich moved to Grove House in Fore Street, where she died a few years later:

Died: At Grove-house, Topsham, Devon, aged 80, Mrs. Margaret Goodrich, relict of the late John G. Esq. of Virginia.[117]

Like many who had spent most of their lives on plantations, Margaret Goodrich's acts of charity at home in England were deemed worthy of public record:

... died, in an advanced age, at her house in Topsham, Mrs Margaret Goodrich, relict of John Goodrich, Esq. late of Virginia, in North America, whose loss will be long and deservedly lamented by her numerous relatives and friends, and seriously felt by the poor, to whom she was a constant and liberal benefactress.[118]

Several of the children of John and Margaret Goodrich became very wealthy. The eldest son William was a partner in a Bristol tobacco and sugar-trading business with his brother-in-law Robert Shedden and together they purchased the 100-acre Spring Hill estate near Cowes in 1794. Perhaps the location reminded them of the county of Isle of Wight in Virginia. The second son John Goodrich (V) lived at Energlyn, near Caerphilly, Wales and became High Sheriff of Glamorganshire in 1798. The daughter Agatha, married to Robert Shedden, became extremely rich. As well as trading with the plantations, the Shedden family also invested directly in sugar plantations in Jamaica.[119]

On the abolition of slavery, compensation was divided between their sons and their grand-daughter Mary.[120]

The survival of the Goodrich name in Topsham rested on the descendants of the youngest son Samuel who married twice after the flight to England, first to Catherine Hare (in 1786) and then to Harriet Juaniz y Echalaz (in 1793). In 1807, Robert Shedden provided for Samuel, his youngest brother-in-law, by purchasing a house in Topsham:[121]

> *all that messuage tenement or dwelling house, with the garden and appurtenances, being part of a tenement commonly known by the name of Rollstones* [in Strand] *lying and being in Topsham formerly the lands and inheritance of Joseph Comer of East Budleigh gent. deceased and now in the possession of* **Samuel Goodrich, Esq as Tenant.**[122]

When Robert Shedden died in 1826, he left £120,000. He bequeathed his house in Gower Street, London to his wife Agatha and included an additional bequest:

> *I give devise and bequeath unto my said dear wife Agatha Wells Shedden her Heirs Executors Administrators and Assigns my small House [Rollstones] and Garden in Topsham in the County of Devon.*

Agatha, the last remaining child of John and Margaret Goodrich, died in 1838. She in turn remembered her brother Samuel's family in her will:[123]

> *Agatha Wells Shedden, widow of Robert Shedden - I give and bequeath my small house and garden with its appurtenances at Topsham in the County of Devon left me by my said late husband Robert Shedden and now occupied by my nephew James Goodrich unto my said nephew James Goodrich his heirs and assigns forever, which bequest I make according to the intention of my said late husband. Signed – 10 Jan 1834.*

James Bridger Goodrich (1789-1836) — m.1815 Sarah Cannings (1789-1854)

- Margaret Bridger Goodrich (1817-1832)
- Catharine Eliza Goodrich (1819-1837)
- Agatha Wells Goodrich (1821-1883) m. 1851 William Williams (1808-1895)
  - Roscoe Shedden Goodrich Williams (1852-1935) m. 1896 Amy Haycroft (b. 1864)
  - Agatha Beatrix Goodrich Williams (1855-1938)
- Robert Shedden Goodrich (b. 1823)
- James Bridger Goodrich (1825-1905) m. 1851 Mary Ann Trout (1832-1864)
  - Robert John Sheddon Goodrich (b. 1852)
  - Evelyn Charlotte Theresa Goodrich (1855-1860)
  - Algernon William Dick Goodrich (1859-1937) m. 1883 Annie Cecilia Bence (d. 1890) m. 1896 not known
  - Agatha Elizabeth Evelyn Goodrich (1862-1887) m. 1878 John William Harcourt Parkin (1852-1936)
- Edward Stratton Goodrich (1827-1859) m. 1850 Martha Burfield
  - Charles Edward Goodrich (1852-1913)
  - Agatha Sarah Goodrich (1853-1905)
  - Elizabeth Mather Goodrich (b. 1856)

James Bridger Goodrich (1789-1836) family tree

The title of Rollstones, the 'small' Shedden house in Topsham purchased with money gained trading with the plantations, thus passed through three generations of the Goodrich family, from Agatha to her brother Samuel and then to Samuel's son James and onto his son James Bridger Goodrich Jnr.

'England's Rose', James Bridger Goodrich in 1858 recorded the opening of the refurbished dry dock, Strand (Topsham Museum)

James Bridger Goodrich Jnr (1825-1906) earned his living as a landscape artist and the above painting is now owned by Topsham Museum.

His sister Agatha Wells Goodrich married William Williams, an artist from Plymouth, and they were living at Rollstones in 1857 with their five-year-old son Roscoe Shedden Goodrich Williams, who grew up to become a landscape artist like his father, under the professional name of S.G. Williams Roscoe.

The family links with planation life were not entirely severed. Two of James Bridger Goodrich Junior's children moved to Jamaica. His eldest son, Robert Shedden Goodrich, lived on the Hampstead Plantation in Trelawney parish. Robert's 17-year-old sister Agatha married John William Harcourt Parkin at Hampstead plantation. John Parkin was educated at a school in St David's Hill, Exeter,[124] and was perhaps a schoolfriend of Robert Goodrich, now his brother-in-law. *Western Times* - Friday 05 July 1878:

> — *Parkin-Goodrich*, — *June 5, by special license, at Hampstead Estate Trelawny, Jamaica, by the Rev. A. Kilburn.* **John William Harcourt Parkin**, *eldest son of J. W. Parkin, Esq., of Catherine Mount Estate, Jamaica, to* **Agatha Elizabeth Evelyn Goodrich**, *only sister of Robert Shedden Goodrich, Esq., of Hampstead Estate, Jamaica, West Indies.*

Agatha Goodrich's new father-in-law John Parkin Snr (1812-1893) lived on the Catherine Mount estate near Montego Bay in post-abolition Jamaica where he was a plantation administrator, magistrate, sometime Custos[125] of St James and an officer in the Western Interior regiment. He visited Topsham a couple of years after the wedding. The 1881 census shows that he, his daughter Kate and younger son Frederick stayed for at least one night, not with Agatha's parents but at Barton Cottage in the High Street, with Barbara Tharp (née Clarke). 10 years earlier, in 1871, Kate Parkin, then a 13-year-old schoolgirl, was living with Barbara at Barton Cottage. A few years later, in 1887, Mr J. Parkin was one of the guests when St Margaret's church was re-consecrated after renovation. The Parkin family were long-standing inhabitants of Jamaica and their marital and friendship links with Topsham are yet another example of how the long fingers of slavery touched many lives.

At the time of the visit to Topsham by John Parkin Snr in 1881, life in Jamaica was changing. The white propertied class still held dominant political positions, though, and the black population, although free for over 40 years, remained poor and disenfranchised.

At the turn of the 20th century, both John W.H. Parkin and Robert S. Goodrich were still living and working in Jamaica, by now both Justices of the Peace and owners or lessees of at least four sugar estates each, all in the north of the island.[126] In 1900 the following announcement appeared in the *Western Times*:

> *MARRIAGES - Mills-Parkin. On the 2nd instant, at the Parish Church, Montego Bay, Jamaica, W.I., by the Rev. J.W. Austin, assisted by the Rev. M.C. Clare, B.A., Andrew MacFarlane Mills, L.R.C.P., and M.R.C.S., England to Agatha Evelyn Louisa, elder daughter of John H. Parkin, Esq., of Catherine Mount, and niece of Robert Shedden Goodrich, late of Topsham, Devon.*[127]

9. Further Links To The Caribbean: *The Gibbs, Sturm, Cadogan, Beare And Thwaites Families*

In the early 1700s a younger son of the Gibbs family, Abraham Gibbs, moved from Pytte farm in Clyst St George to Shapter Street in Topsham. His sons and grandsons used their extended family, friends, and religious and business connections to establish a trading network. They owned plantations, invested in slaving voyages, provided goods to the plantations in the Caribbean and the American mainland, and dealt in slave-produced goods.

Abraham Gibbs's elder son John (1725-1774) grew up in Shapter Street, Topsham and became a merchant mariner in the salt-cod triangular trade. Ships would leave England with commodities for the fishermen living and working in Newfoundland. There they loaded up with barrels of salted cod for sale in the Mediterranean. Inferior fish was also loaded and on the second leg of the journey the ships sailed to Virginia, the Carolinas or the West Indies, where plantation owners bought the poor-quality fish to feed enslaved workers. The vessels were then reloaded with sugar or rice for sale along with the top-quality cod in the Mediterranean. Between 1741 and 1763 John captained *Experiment, John and Elizabeth* and other vessels, making at least one round trip to Newfoundland, the Carolinas and Maryland then onto the West Indies.[128] His sons Jack (b.1755), William (1757-1830), Abraham (1758-1816), Lyle (1761-1839) and Thomas (1767-1796) all became merchants and businessmen in that trade.

Jack and William were primarily based in Bristol, Abraham in Livorno and Naples, Lyle in Genoa and Thomas in Quebec, and together they exported cloth from Exeter and salt fish, sugar and rice from the Americas, selling their goods in markets in the Mediterranean.

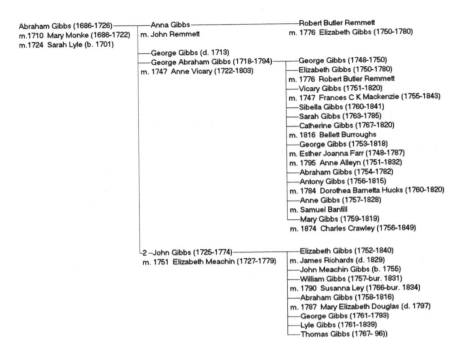

Gibbs family tree

Abraham's other son George (1718-1794) was a surgeon rather than a merchant, but his four sons Vicary (1751-1820), George (1753-1818), Abraham (1752-1782) and Antony (1756-1815) worked alongside their cousins to develop the family's trading network. Vicary studied law and was appointed Solicitor General in 1805.[129] He used his political influence to support his family against the abolition of slavery. George became a partner in a Bristol business, importing commodities from the Mediterranean and the Baltic and exporting them to the Caribbean, American plantations and Newfoundland.[130] As Master of the Merchant Venturers in 1790, he led the Bristol campaign against the abolition of slavery. Abraham and Antony were cloth merchants in Exeter and Antony branched out into banking, shipping and insurance.

The family married strategically – George married first the daughter of a prominent slave trader and later Anne Alleyne, whose family had extensive plantations in Barbados. (Some 80 years before, a daughter of Charles and Mary Buttall of the Topsham sugar-refining family had also married into the Alleyne family in Barbados.) George's cousin Betsy married his business partner and Betsy later claimed compensation relating to a plantation in Jamaica. Abraham married into a consular family and his daughter inherited a plantation in St Kitts.

In 1816, William returned to Topsham to live in the family house in Shapter Street, where he became a pillar of the local community. He died in 1831 and was buried in Topsham. Following his death, the family house was sold. Two years later slavery ended and the Gibbs family was awarded compensation for loss of over 300 enslaved people on their plantations in Barbados and Jamaica. They never returned to Topsham but re-invested their considerable business profits in the Bristol docks, the Clifton Bridge, the Great Western Railway and other infrastructure projects as well as industry. [131]

Quartermaster-Serjeant Frederick Sturm was a German national, born c. 1758, who served in the British Army from around 1775 until 1818. He was a tall (5 feet 9 inches), red-haired man who married a Topsham widow in 1814 and moved to Taylor's Lane (now Station Road).

Sturm claimed that he was in Grenada twice: from around 1779 to 1783 as a French prisoner, and again from 1788 to 1793 as a member of the 67th (South Hampshire) Regiment of Foot. This was about the time Alexander Hamilton inherited the Samaritan sugar estate from his brother Robert, and Samuel Mitchell was living and working on the island.

Frederick Sturm never owned land or enslaved people, but he would have been witness to the brutal conditions on the plantations and was a professional soldier charged with maintaining British rule in the colonies. He died in 1844 and he and his wife are buried in Topsham. His son William became a blacksmith and lived in White Street. He and his wife are also buried in Topsham.

The 'Will of Ward Cadogan [1772-1833] formerly of Barbadoes [sic] and late of Northbrook House near Exeter, Devon'[132] was made in

1831. (The site of Northbrook became a golf course and the grounds of Exeter crematorium but in 1831 it was part of Topsham parish.)

Cadogan was born in Barbados, where his family had lived since 1679. He owned plantations in the parish of St Lucy and resided in Bridgetown where he operated as a merchant, selling goods and property, and arranging shipments and maritime insurance.[133] In 1810, Cadogan announced that he was:

> *Intending to take passage for England in the first Fleet … and will sell for cash, at reduced prices, the following articles, viz. Deal lumber and oak Staves, Wood Hoops, Nails, Candles, Soap, Butter, and Salt.*[134]

He settled at first in Bristol but in his 1831 will he refers to himself as 'of Topsham'. He had settled at Northbrook House and begun to establish himself by doing good works. In 1832, he contributed £5 to a fund held by the Exeter Board of Health to support poor families suffering as a result of a cholera outbreak in the city,[135] and in March 1833 he provided Indian Corn seed for the Devon and Exeter Society to distribute to local Cottagers.

In August that year, Ward Cadogan suddenly died. He was buried in St Margaret's churchyard and a memorial was placed in the church. He does not appear to have owned Northbrook House but to have leased it from Evangelical Anglicans in Exeter.

Memorial to Ward Cadogan in St Margaret's, Topsham

He left his Barbados estates and the *'negroes and slaves, live and dead stock on them'* to his daughter Sarah and his grandchildren, together with mortgages over other estates and monetary legacies. He also left a small legacy of £50 to *'my black servant John Day'*. John may have been living at Northbrook in 1833 but does not appear in any known records.

In 1834, Cadogan's wife, citing an address in St James, Westminster sought compensation for the loss of 515 enslaved workers on the Harrow, Pickerings and Crab Hill Estates in Barbados. She received awards totalling £11,248. Probably drawing on this compensation and his personal legacy from his grandfather, Ward Cadogan's grandson Cadogan Hodgson Cadogan (1827-1886) set about renovating Brinkburn Priory in Northumberland, now owned by English Heritage.

James Beare claimed for the loss of five enslaved workers in Grenada and was awarded £106 12s 11d in compensation. On 26 February 1842, the *Western Times* reported that *Jas. Beare Esq., formerly of Topsham*, had died in Grenada on 4 January.[136]

There is, as yet, no further information on this family.

In 1837, recently married John Thwaites and Hester, his widowed mother, both living in Topsham, received unexpected windfalls that allowed them to live comfortably for the rest of their lives.

The source of the money was John Bolton, the son of a Lancashire apothecary, who went to the Caribbean island of St Vincent in 1773. He soon became a plantation owner, merchant and slave trader, eventually operating out of Liverpool and involved in at least 69 slave voyages. He retired to a mansion (Storrs Hall) in the Lake District and when he died in 1837 he left a fortune of £180,000.

John Bolton had an older sister Mary who married Robert Thwaites of Liverpool, perhaps a colleague or employee of her brother. They had a son John who in turn married Esther (Hester) Burnford in 1807. Within a year, John and Hester Thwaites had a son of their own and they named him John Bolton Thwaites in honour of his prosperous great-uncle. A few months later, they moved to Topsham and John Bolton Thwaites grew up in the town. In 1833, he visited Somerset with a Topsham friend to marry the daughter of a cleric.

Four years later John Bolton, slave merchant of Liverpool, left an annuity of £200 p.a. to *Mrs* [Hester] *Thwaites, widow of* [his nephew] *John Thwaites late of Topsham in Devon*, and several thousand pounds to his great-nephew, John Bolton Thwaites.

John Bolton Thwaites was able to use this windfall, profit from his great-uncle's slaving activities, to buy Hart House, set in 6.5 acres of land in Burnham-on-Sea in Somerset, near his wife's family home.

Hart House, Burnham-on-sea (1898)

He became a Justice of the Peace, Chairman of the local Board of Health and local President of the Lifeboat Association. He died there in 1892, leaving the remains of his fortune to his own children, Frederick Bolton Thwaites, gentleman, Rev. Henry G. Thwaites and Ellen M. A. Thwaites, spinster.

The legacy from John Bolton *West India and South American merchant, slave trader, and slave owner,*[137] derived from enslavement, allowed John Bolton Thwaites and his family to enjoy a life of leisure and genteel luxury.

10. 'Invisible' in Topsham

Throughout this booklet, there have been just a few, tantalising glimpses of the enslaved people who lived on the plantations but whose stories can only be known through the lives of the people who enslaved them.

The same is true of black people who visited or lived in Topsham during the time of slavery. We know of them only through church records, the graves in the cemetery and occasionally the names of the people who enslaved them. These are the meagre records:

11 June 1715	baptism of Ann Avery. A Black, aged 37
18 June 1715	burial of Ann Avery, a black aged 37 [linked to Sir John Colleton, 3rd Bart]
6 February 1771	burial of Isaac Primus, a Black, aged 27 [servant to Sir John Colleton, 4th Bart]
7 August 1783	burial of Abigail Wallay, a black woman, buried by the parish
11 January 1786	burial of Charles Lewis, a Negro servant
11 March 1786	baptism of Thomas Greenock [adult negro servant of Thomas Hall]
18 May 1787	baptism of Mary Wallay, an adult Negro woman, and Fanny Wallay, her daughter, a Negro girl
13 December 1805	burial of John Williams, a negro [from Demerara]
7 January 1809	burial of Mary Williams, Widow, a Negro woman

Before emancipation in 1833, the status of black people away from the Caribbean was complex. Enslaved Africans could be bought and sold at will in the colonies, but at the same time there were free black people living in England with quite sizeable populations in London and the large ports. However, most people of African origin came with slaveholders from the plantations to work as servants in households maintained at home in England.

Ann Avery came to Topsham around the time of the Buttall sugar refinery and when William Upcott was shipping sugar from Barbados. She was enslaved to Sir John Colleton, 3rd Baronet (1669-1754), whose grandfather was responsible for taking the brutal Slave Codes from Barbados to the Carolinas.

Sir John was a *planter merchant* with 27,000 acres of rice plantations worked by many enslaved people in Colleton County, South Carolina. He was considered to be the sixth most wealthy Exeter citizen and he divided his time between his plantations in Carolina and his house in Withycombe Raleigh near Exmouth. In England he is remembered for introducing magnolia trees from his plantation and a blue plaque in Exmouth describes him as *retired Administrator.*

Ann Avery almost certainly worked in the house and she must have been baptised on her deathbed as she was buried a week later, aged just 37. Sir John visited Carolina around 1715, so perhaps they were about to leave England when Ann became ill.

Isaac Primus was enslaved by another generation of the same family. Sir John Colleton, 4th Baronet (1738-1778), lived mainly at Fairlawn, the family mansion in Carolina and visited England only occasionally. Isaac Primus was probably born into slavery in South Carolina and he lived to be only 27 years old. The Colleton name lives on in Exmouth where the magnolia flower is incorporated into the town coat of arms and in the names of streets in both Exmouth and Exeter.

It is likely, although by no means certain, that legally free black servants like Charles Lewis, who died in 1786, would have lived in similar conditions to the white servants in the household. Whether he received wages at the normal rate or was allowed the freedom to live independently or to marry as he chose is not known. Advertisements about fugitives and the records of court cases show that some black servants were held in conditions of enslavement and some were violently abused.

Abigail Wallay died in Topsham three years before Charles Lewis. Perhaps they arrived with John and Mary Goodrich, who moved into a house in Strand around 1783. We can suppose that Abigail and Mary Wallay were related and we know that Mary had a daughter Fanny. Abigail was buried by the parish. Four years after Abigail died, Mary and Fanny, 'a girl', were baptised in St Margaret's church. They were not buried in Topsham, so perhaps they moved or were taken elsewhere when a family moved on.

Thomas Greenock was employed as a servant and was baptised in Topsham but nothing more is known of him or his employer, Thomas Hall.

John and Mary Williams are the last people listed. They were presumably husband and wife but we know nothing more except that they came from Demerara, a colony with plantations and enslaved people on the northern coast of South America.

On 1 May 1807, four months after Mary Williams died, the transportation of enslaved people from Africa (but not the owning of them on plantations) was abolished by parliament. No more Africans would be trafficked aboard British ships. *Kitty's Amelia* had sailed from Liverpool on 27 April 1807 and was the last legal slave voyage by a British vessel. Five years later, Topsham abolitionists met in St Margaret's vestry room to organise petitioning against slavery itself.

11. Topsham Voices for Abolition

The ending of slavery in the British colonies was a lengthy process, at first aiming to halt the trafficking of Africans to the Americas, and then moving towards freeing people who were already enslaved.[138] During the years of campaigning for the hearts and minds of the public, meetings took place in halls and churches throughout the country and petitions were sent to the government. In 1792 alone, over 500 petitions were sent to parliament, at least 12 coming from towns in Devon, including Topsham.[139]

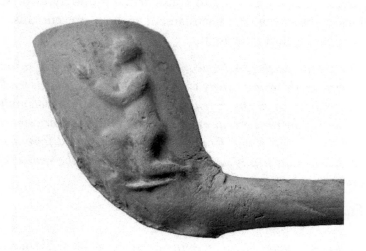

Clay pipe, found in 6 Lower Shapter Street, depicts kneeling slave and standing figure of Liberty (Topsham Museum)

At a meeting in the Salutation Inn, presumably in the upstairs Assembly Room, the *'inhabitants of the town and parish of Topsham'* almost unanimously agreed and signed a *Petition to Parliament for the Abolition on the AFRICAN SLAVE TRADE*. The petition stated:

your Petitioners cannot know that very considerable Numbers of their Fellow Creatures are trepanned or forced from their native Country and tenderest Connections and subjected to a capricious, rigorous, and involuntary Servitude, without feeling a Conviction that the Exercise of the African Slave Trade is injurious to the natural and inherent Rights and Privileges of Mankind. 6 March 1792.[140]

The petition came before the House of Commons four days later[141] but it took another 15 years for legislation to be enacted. Eventually, from 1 May 1807, the *sale, barter, or transfer of slaves* was made illegal in British colonies. While the government had abolished the transatlantic trade, there was a self-sustaining population of enslaved people already in the colonies and slavery itself continued until 1834.

By 1814 there was concern that there might be a revival of the African Slave Trade and a meeting was held in the vestry of St Margaret's Church on 4 July to consider the propriety of presenting petitions to both houses of Parliament to help prevent this.[142] The first of seven resolutions stated:

That this meeting, adverting with the deepest regret to an article in the recent Treaty of Peace with France, which tends to promote an extensive renewal of the Slave Trade, solemnly abolished by the Legislation of this country, feel it incumbent on them, as men and Christians, to use their most strenuous exertions consistently with the laws, to prevent the revival of such a disgraceful and inhuman traffic.

The final resolution was:

That the thanks of this meeting be given to W. Wilberforce, Esq. M.P. and Thomas Clarkson, Esq. for their unwearied exertion to effect the total abolition of the Slave Trade. That these resolutions be advertised in the three Exeter papers.

The meeting was chaired by the rector, the Rev. James Carrington and a committee was appointed including Carrington, Rev. John Follet, James Patch, Esq., John Palmer, Robert Cross, Richard Harrison, Gilbert Mudge, Thomas L. Brown, Francis Trobridge and H. Hellett.

One gentleman of note in the town, Robert Davy, was conspicuous by his absence from this meeting. He was 51 by then but was hale and hearty and lived for another 48 years. Possibly he was away from home, but this might reflect a family view against prohibition of the slave trade as the Davys had extensive investments in Jamaica.[143]

In 1788, Rev. James Carrington's eldest daughter Elizabeth, then 16 years old, had married William Pennell whose family owned a cod-trading business in Topsham and Newfoundland. At first, William managed a branch of the family firm, but in 1817 he was appointed British Consul in Bahia, now part of Brazil.

Bahia was the major destination for Portuguese slave ships, bringing Africans to work on sugar, tobacco and cacao plantations in Brazil. Portugal had no wish to follow Britain in abolishing its slave trade, but in 1815 agreed not to procure enslaved people from parts of Africa north of the equator.

As British consul, William Pennell was tasked with verifying Portugal's observance of the treaties and investigating the continuing plight of those already enslaved in Brazil.[144] Letters he sent to the British foreign secretary show his attention to detail. He noted that most of the enslaved people imported into Brazil came from the 'prohibited District' south of the equator, and he explained that high mortality amongst those bought in Mozambique encouraged traders to buy illegally further north. He also suggested that capturing ships and freeing people who had been enslaved only resulted in increased trading on the Guinea Coast.

Charles Pennell, possibly a son of William, was British Consul in Salvador in 1827 when he reported that Brazilian sugar planters calculated that it was cheaper to import enslaved adults than to pay the costs of raising black children to an age when they became productive workers.[145]

On 10 August 1837 there were reports of meetings in six Devon towns, including Topsham, to celebrate the 30th anniversary of abolition of the African transport ships.[146] The following year, on 1 August 1838, slavery itself was finally abolished. Emancipation came later in other countries and their colonies – Holland in 1863, the US in 1865, Spain in 1886 and Brazil in 1888.

12. Conclusion

Research into links between Topsham and the Caribbean is ongoing. At the time of writing, it is unclear how much of the compensation money and other profit from the plantations made its way into the fabric of the town. The families who settled here from the Caribbean moved on and none remained after 1900. The descendants of merchants and other businessmen who profited from trading with the plantations have also moved away. The only known legacies remaining in the town are their statuary memorials and graves, their contributions to church restoration and the charitable funds left by Barbara Tharp. It is possible that infrastructure funded by Robert Davy (including Topsham Lock) and the homes built by his sons (Riversmeet and Grove Hill) together with the enhancement of The Retreat by Alexander Hamilton were partly funded by money from the plantations, but this is entirely speculative. Today, geographical names recall Sir Alexander Hamilton and Robert Davy. The others are largely forgotten.

It is far from clear why, during the time of slavery and after, so many plantation owners made their homes in the West Country, including Topsham. One possible reason is that emigrants who were originally from the area maintained local family and business links. Some of the disaffected Royalists from Devon and Somerset migrated to Barbados after the Civil War and then developed business interests on other islands in the Caribbean. These families may have persuaded other friends in the Colonial plantocracy to join them in retirement in Devon.

There were advantages other than friendship. The mild climate was relatively kind to those who had spent years in the Tropics. Exeter was a reliable source of goods to furnish homes, provision plantations and clothe slaves. There was easy access to finance and banking –

the Baring, Duntze and Praed families had started banks in Exeter and had always been ready to offer loans. There were local boarding schools where the sons of planters not quite able to afford Eton could be educated. There was also a time advantage. Ships departing for the Caribbean from ports in the South West could gain a two-week advantage on ships departing from Channel ports further east. With an open sea route to the south, they could use the Westerlies on the first leg to Madeira and then swing over to Barbados and beyond. As the port of Exeter, Topsham was a small town where former planters could blend quietly into the gentry and enjoy semi-rural life with local amenities close to hand.

In the Caribbean islands, the few remaining written records are gradually being digitised, researched and shared and it is possible that more information about the enslaved people with links to Topsham may eventually emerge.

Further Reading

Many voices and perspectives have been omitted or ignored in the past. Virtually no first-hand slave narratives from the Caribbean remain and there are just a few from the late 19th century United States. Some of these records are mentioned in the text. Other sources of further information are listed below:

Slave censuses from the early 1800s are held at the National Archives at Kew.

Centre for the Study of the Legacies of British Slavery, UCL, online database: https://www.ucl.ac.uk/lbs

Professor Sir Hilary Beckles, *The First Black Slave Society*, University of the West Indies Press, 2016

Guy Grannum, *Tracing Your Caribbean Ancestors*, Bloomsbury, 2012

Todd Gray, *Devon and the Slave Trade*, The Mint Press, 2007

Footnotes

1 'Legacies of British Slave-Ownership Project, Centre for the Study of the Legacies of British Slavery, University College London. This database is in the public domain: https://www.ucl.ac.uk/lbs/

2 Ottobah Cugoano, *Narrative of the Enslavement of a native of Africa,* printed by James Bullock, Fleet Street, London,1787; Olaudah Equiano, *The Interesting Narrative of the Life of Olaudah Equiano,* 1789; Ashton Warner, *The Narrative of Ashton Warner of St Vincent, F. Estley and A. H. Davis, London, 1831;* and Mary Prince, *History of Mary Prince, A West Indian Slave Related by Herself, F. Estly and A.H. Davis, London, 1831*

3 'On the causes of the African Slave Trade', paper by Luis Angeles, Senior Lecturer in Economics, Adam Smith Business School, University of Glasgow, 2012

4 Richard Hakluyt (c.1552-1616), an Elizabethan travel writer. He noted that Hawkins 'profited by the sale of slaves'. When John Hawkins was knighted, he included a bound slave wearing a necklace and earrings on his new coat of arms.

5 Neil Irvin Painter, *The Guardian*, 14 August 2019

6 D.B. Davis, *Inhuman Bondage,* OUP, 2006, p3

7 Hugh Thomas, *History of the Atlantic Slave Trade,* chapter 11, 1997

8 David Olusoga, 'Britain's Forgotten Slave Owners' BBC series 2016

9 'What Africans got for their slaves: A master list of European trade goods'. *History in Africa* Vol. 22, CUP. 1995. https://www.jstor.org/stable/3171906

10   Ottobah Cugoano, *Narrative of the Enslavement of a native of Africa,* printed by James Bullock, Fleet Street, London,1787; Olaudah Equiano, *The Interesting Narrative of the Life of Olaudah Equiano,* 1789

11   Ashton Warner, *The Narrative of Ashton Warner of St Vincent, F. Estley and A. H. Davis, London, 1831;* and Mary Prince, *History of Mary Prince, A West Indian Slave Related by Herself, F. Estly and A.H. Davis, London, 1831*

12   David Olusoga, 'Britain's Forgotten Slave Owners', BBC 2016

13   David Brion Davis, *Inhuman Bondage: The Rise and Fall of Slavery in the New World,* OUP, 2006. p. 238

14   Marquis of Sligo, Governor of Jamaica, 16 August, 1834

15   *Jamaica Royal Gazette* 16 August 1834, reprinted in *Sherborne Mercury* 6 October 1834

16   slavevoyages.org

17   Tattersfield, Nigel, *The Forgotten Trade,* Jonathan Cape, 1991, p.282-6

18   An agent responsible for the actual procurement of slaves from the interior.

19   Francis Moore, *Travels into the Inland Parts of Africa,* printed by Edward Gale, London, 1738. (Special Collections, Alderman Library, University of Virginia)

20   'The Royal Adventurers in England', G F Zook, *Journal of African History,* Univ. of Chicago Press, Apr 1919

21   Olaudah Equiano, *The Interesting Narrative of the Life of Olaudah Equiano,* 1789

22   ibid.

23   *Economic History Review,* August 2001, Wiley

24   Memorial of Colonel John Toogood to the Court of Directors of the East India Company concerning the two 'princes of Delagoa', September 1720: IOR/E/1/11 ff. 326-328v.

25   British Library Records

26 Tattersfield, Nigel, *The Forgotten Trade,* Jonathan Cape, 1991, p.295-6

27 *The Christian Monitors, The Church of England and the Age of Benevolence,* Brent S Sirola, Yale University Press, 2014

28 Professor Sir Hilary Beckles, University of the West Indies, in conversation with David Olusoga

29 Ashton Warner, transcribed by Susan Strickland, *The Narrative of Ashton Warner of St Vincent,* London, 1831

30 Sheridan, Richard B, 1974, *Sugar and Slavery, 1623-1775,* pp.112-18

31 UCL compensation records: William Harding, buried 11 May 1832 in St Philip, Barbados, recorded as of "Buttal's, St George's".

32 Marriage to Mary Bromley in1669, Barbados Marriages, Vol I, 1643-1800, St John Parish

33 Topsham Deeds, Devon Heritage Centre, Doc. DD.100260

34 Clark E.A.G., *The Ports of the Exe Estuary,* University of Exeter Press, 1960

35 Maunder, Peter, *Tiverton Cloth, 1475-1815,* p.197, Short Run Press, 2018.

36 The property was Conway House in Lower Shapter Street, Topsham.

37 Will of Samuel Buttall: PRO, PCC Prob 11/594, 1723. The land in Carolina adjoined the Edisto River, seven miles from New London.

38 *London Gazette,* 28 September 1723.

39 Topsham Deeds, DRO

40 Eliot, Howard, *Eliot Papers, No.1, John Eliot of London, Merchant, 1735-1813,* p.18, Pub: E. Hicks Jnr., London, 1895.

41 Will of Mary Hodges PRO, PCC Prob 11/737, 2 Feb 1744

42 A more detailed description of this episode is given in the book *Thomas Glass* by Alick Cameron, Devon Books, 1996. It includes the full texts of the letters between Glass, Mary Hodges and her son George.

[43] Polwhele, R., 1793-1806, *The History of Devonshire*, 2, 208fn (Monograph).

[44] Ibid.

[45] Exeter and its neighbourhood under George III, by Robert Dymond,*Exeter Flying Post*, February 5, 1879.

[46] *The Times*, Monday 21 August 1786: St James's, August 18th. The King was this day pleased to confer the honour of Knighthood on Alexander Hamilton, Esq. Sheriff of the county of Devon.

[47] Gavin Smith Survey, 1821-24

[48] Swete 1792, vol. 8, 146

[49] T*he London Gazette* - 19 March 1811 Issue:16465 Page:528

[50] *The London Gazette* - 28 October 1828, Issue 18518, page 1953

[51] *Western Times,* Saturday 16 July 1853

[52] Barge Yard, a handsome open Place, and very well inhabited, having some large Houses at the upper end; Bucklersbury turneth out of Cheapside, and runneth on the back side of the Poultry, unto Walbrook: A Street very well built, and inhabited by Tradesmen, especially Drugsters and Furriers. *Strype's Survey of London*.

[53] The French had controlled the island from 1672 until 1762, when the British invaded during the Seven Years War. Under the Treaty of Paris in 1763, Grenada passed into British hands.

[54] Thomas Jefferys, London, 1760s

[55] Chisholm, C, *Cases of Ruptured Spleen and Liver by External Injury, with Remarks thereon.* Edinburgh Medical and Surgical Journal, vol.7, 1811, 257.

[56] Devon Heritage Centre 1926 B/B/L/2/10

[57] *Morning Post* - Wednesday 15 September 1802

[58] *Exeter Flying Post* – Thursday 07 February 1805.

[59] Registers of Births, Marriages and Deaths Devon Presbyterian Piece RG4/0965: Exeter, Bow Meeting (Presbyterian) - Samuel Mitchel, Esq., Aged 55, buried on his Estate at Newport, Feb 17th, 1805, J. Manning.

60 'The lack of white women helped to provide an impetus for white men of all social groups to take non-White mistresses. Referred to euphemistically as 'housekeepers', these concubines were often enslaved women. Since legal status was inherited from one's mother, the children of these enslaved mistresses and sexual partners were born into slavery regardless of the legal status of the father. Higman (*Slave population and economy* p. 139) has estimated that between 1829 and 1832, white men fathered more than nine per cent of all registered newly-born slaves. Concubinage often involved cohabitation and, as Barbara Bush has stated (*Slave Women in Caribbean Society 1650-1838* Oxford, James Curry 1990 p.111) was regarded as an integral part of plantation life, inextricably woven into the social fabric. Liaisons between white men and non-white women could be reciprocal and long-term, but less consensual sexual interaction was far more commonplace.' (wrap.warwick.ac.uk)

61 The *Western Times,* Saturday 02 November 1833

62 In the possession of a relation, Rev. H.A. Wright of Strand, Topsham c.1905

63 *A Genealogical and Heraldic History of the Landed Gentry of Great Britain & Ireland,* Sir Bernard Burke C.B., LL.D., Vol. II, 1871, p. 1369, Harrison, Pall Mall, London

64 In 1816, the *Exeter Flying Post* reported that a game shooting certificate was issued to William V, and in 1819 both young men received game certificates.

65 *Exeter Flying Post,* Thursday 25 July 1822

66 *Exeter Flying Post* - Thursday 17 June 1824

67 Will of John Horlock dated 4 October, 1824 mentions "my nephews (the sons of my sister Mrs Mary Tharp widow) named William and Thomas Tharp are all now in France."

68 PCC will PROB 11/1764/215.

69 Ashton Warner, transcribed by Susan Strickland, *The Narrative of Ashton Warner of St Vincent,* London, 1831

70 *Royal Gazette of Jamaica,* 12 July 1794

[71] Annual report of the Committee of the Baptist Missionary Society 1832, Yale University

[72] The *Exeter Flying Post*, Thursday 14 August 1834

[73] The fact that Benjamin is listed as "youngest son" of William Mary in this will of 1834 indicates that their actual youngest son, Thomas Reid Tharp II (b.1828), has died.

[74] Will of James Clarke proved 1823, National Archives PROB 11/1667/471

[75] One of four miniatures advertised for sale by Bearnes, Exeter

[76] Tapley-Soper, Harry, Transcript of Topsham Parish Register: p.752: Schedule of Memorial Inscriptions in Topsham Churchyard

[77] *Exeter and Plymouth Gazette* - Saturday 29 March 1856

[78] *Exeter and Plymouth Gazette* - Saturday 19 December 1835; Died: On Dec. 11, Topsham, John Ben. Tharp, aged 14 years and 7 months, third son of the late William Tharp, Esq., of the Island of Jamaica.

[79] Elwes had married the sister of his previous father-in-law's, brother's wife!

[80] John Martin Birom was the godson (and possibly the natural illegitimate son) of John Horlock, brother of Mary Harrison Tharp (1754-1854). He was educated by John Horlock, and would have known Thomas Tharp (and probably his own future wife Elizabeth) from childhood.

[81] Harriet Crosley married William Brandt Brown, in 1803, after the death of her husband Thomas Ventum.

[82] Topsham Cemetery - HOE, Harriet Harcourt, age 87, Topsham Parish, Loc.No.699 (reopened), buried 26/4/1875.

[83] *Exeter and Plymouth Gazette* Daily Telegrams - Wednesday 06 November 1878

[84] *Western Times* - Saturday 25 August 1849 - Aug. 23, Topsham, by the Rev. H. Thorp, B. H. Tharp, Esq., of the Island of Jamaica, to Ellen Louisa, the eldest daughter of Mr. Hy. Paul, of the former place.

85 *Monumental Inscriptions of Jamaica,* Philip Wright, Society of Genealogists (Great Britain), 1966, p.230.

86 *Hampshire Chronicle* 13 Sep 1851.

87 *Exeter Flying Post* 25 February 1799, quoted in Clive N Ponsford, *Shipbuilding on the Exe,* Devon and Cornwall Record Society, 1988.

88 *Jamaica Planter* carried 20 guns and was licensed to carry 45 armed men. The convoys, guns and armed men reflect the dangers to ships crossing the Atlantic.

89 *Medina* was a 424-ton ship and it carried 18 guns.

90 Gillian Allan, 'Two Devon families in Jamaica: a local association with slavery', Maritime South West No. 21 (2008) p.8

91 G.J.G. Davy, 'The Davy Family: Gaius 1633 to Ebony Rae 2012' (Xlibris, 2013).

92 Gillian Allen, 'Slavery and two Ottery St Mary families', *Heritage - Journal of the Ottery St Mary Heritage Society* No. 30 Summer 2009 pp. 3-5

93 As Martin Weiler explains, they named their plantations after their Devon homes. http://www.jamaicanfamilysearch.com/Samples2/Heavitree2.htm.

94 Institute of Jamaica, 15N, 4576, M300, viewed by Gillian Allen in September 2011

95 The wording 'Ran away' deliberately suggests that the law was on the side of slaveholding society, and that seeking freedom was a criminal act.

96 *Royal Gazette of Jamaica.* Saturday 29 November 1794

97 Will of Rebecca Davy of Wear, Topsham. Public Record Office, PROB 11/1725

98 Baptism of John in Exminster, 9 August 1801, George Thomas in Topsham 13 June 1803, Frances Portbury and Eliza Powell in Alphington 21 November 1808, when George Thomas was baptised for a second time. The residence of the parents was noted as being Exminster.

99 Gillian Allen, 'Two Devon Families in Jamaica', *Maritime South West,* No. 21, 2008

100 National Archive, Ref: T71/68

101 Index of Baptisms, Parish of Manchester, Vol 1/p.139, Island Record Office, Jamaica

102 The Green Pond mentioned in the table was in Manchester, as distinct from Green Pond, St James, owned by the Tharp family.

103 Advert in *Royal Gazette of Jamaica,* 23 Feb 1828.

104 Literally *Keeper of the rolls*

105 Heavy Tree (or Heavitree) first appears in the Jamaica records in 1838.

106 Gillian Allen, 'Two Devon Families in Jamaica', *Maritime South West,* No. 21, 2008

107 Olaudah Equiano, *The Interesting Narrative of the Life of Olaudah Equiano,* 1789

108 Boddie, John Bennett, *Seventeenth-century Isle of Wight County, Virginia,* pp. 222-4

109 These ships were between 25 and 50 tons.

110 Virginia Historical Society, 'Collections of the Virginia Historical Society', Vol. 10, p. 46

111 Curtis, George M. 'The Goodrich Family and the Revolution in Virginia, 1774-1776', *The Virginia Magazine of History and Biography,* vol. 84, no. 1, 1976, pp. 49–74. JSTOR, www.jstor.org/stable/4248008.

112 Letter to George Germain, Secretary of State for America

113 Tormey p. 98

114 Symons and Glanville, in Tapley-Soper, H.

115 Deed of release, 25 March 1793 - Devon Heritage Centre, Pearse box 146.

116 *Exeter Flying Post,* Thursday, September 4, 1806; issue 2237

117 *Gentleman's Magazine* for the year MDCCCX (1810) May - Obituary

118 *Trewman's Exeter Flying Post* or *Plymouth and Cornish Advertiser* (Exeter, England), Thursday, April 26, 1810; Issue 2325

119 Stewart Castle plantation (288 enslaved), Flower Hill (285 enslaved), Westmoreland 66 (245 enslaved), Trelawney 123 (140 enslaved), Trelawney 122 (61 enslaved)

120 Daughter of his deceased son, Bartlett Bridger Shedden

121 Purchased from James William Fallon, whose wife was a member of Topsham's well-known Brand family

122 Indenture, 13 June 1807. The property has been identified as at 20-21 Strand.

123 Will of Agnes Wells Shedden, widow of Gower Street, Middlesex, PROB 11/1896.

124 RG10/2065/52/14

125 The Custos was the government representative and chief magistrate of the parish, in this case St James.

126 1900 Jamaica Handbook (sugar estates in cultivation): WH PARKIN St James: Anchovy and Eden, Content (lessee), Catherine Mount, Leogan (attorney for RS Goodrich); Hanover: Tryall

127 *Western Times,* Friday 9 February, 1900

128 Lloyds Lists and Registers, 1741-44, 1749-50

129 MP for Totnes in 1805 and member for Great Bedwyn in Wiltshire in 1807, Vicary held the post of Attorney General in both the Portland and Perceval governments.

130 The firm was later renamed Munckley, Gibbs & Richards

131 We are grateful to Elizabeth Neill for informing this section on the Gibbs family and their links with the Caribbean.

132 Will of Ward Cadogan, PROB 10/7423/14, December 1833, The National Archives, Kew

133 Notice announcing the Barbados Insurance Association, 'formed for the purpose of taking risks on vessels' and including Ward Cadogan amongst the underwriters, *Barbados and Bridge-Town Gazette,* 25.8.1812

[134] *Barbados Mercury and Bridge-Town Gazette*, 2.1.1810

[135] *Exeter and Plymouth Gazette*, 25.8.1832

[136] Also reported in West Indies Obituaries in *The Gentleman's Magazine OR Monthly Intelligencer*, 1842, Vol. 18, p. 223

[137] Entry for John Bolton, *Oxford Dictionary of National Biography*, OUP

[138] *History of the Transatlantic Slave Trade*, Hugh Thomas, 1997, Chapter 23

[139] *Devon and the Slave Trade*, Todd Gray, Mint Press 2007, p172

[140] Trewman's *Exeter Flying Post*, 8 March 1792, cited in www. exetermemories.co.uk>pubs>salutation and by Gillian Allen 'Two Devon Families in Jamaica', *Maritime South West*, No. 21, 2008

[141] 'Journal of the House of Commons' (1792) p552, cited in *Devon and the Slave Trade*, Todd Gray, Mint Press, 2007, pp.172 and 227

[142] *Exeter Flying Post* - Thursday 07 July 1814

[143] Gillian Allen, 'Two Devon Families in Jamaica', *Maritime South West*, No. 21, 2008

[144] As an indication of the complexity of Britain's relationship with slavery, William Pennell and his family lived in the elegant district of Victoria, with stunning views of the bay of Bahia, and his house and gardens were maintained by people enslaved by him. The journal of Maria Graham, 1821, records a soirée in the garden house or gazebo of Consul Pennell which 'literally overhang[s] the bay . . . the English are all served by slaves, indeed.' 'The British Community of 19th Century Bahia: public and private lives', Louise Guenther, Working Paper CBS-32-02, University of Oxford Centre for Brazilian Studies, 2001-2.

[145] David Brion Davis, *Inhuman Bondage: The Rise and Fall of Slavery in the New World*, OUP, 2006

[146] 'Local Black History: A Beginning in Devon', Lucy MacKeith, 2003, p20

Other Museum titles

Topsham: An account of its streets and buildings, Topsham Society, 2005, revised 2014

Holman's: A family business of shipbuilders, shipowners and insurers form 1832, D. Clement, 2006

Dorothy Holman: A life, L. Neal, 2006

Topsham Inns, Colin Piper, 2010

Topsham, A small scale history, C. Oboussier et al., 2012

Salmon Fishing on the Exe, M. Patrick, 2012

Topsham and the Quay Railway, Topsham Museum Society, 2013

Cygnet: The story of a boat, D. Clement, 2013

Topsham's Suffragists 1911-1913, P. and M. Patrick, 2013

Vivien Leigh: The Topsham connection, L. Ronchetti, 2013

Topsham Remembered, Topsham Museum Oral History Group, 2013

HMS Terror: A Topsham ship, L. Ronchetti, D. Clement, E. Williams-Hawkes, 2014

Crossing the Exe, A. Adcock and M. Dant, 2015

War Comes to Topsham, R. Hatch and M. Grimshaw, 2016

Topsham to Newfoundland, T. Colvin and J. Pearson, 2017

Churches of Topsham, P. Quaife, M. Patrick and church representatives

Countess Wear Paper Mill, L. Ronchetti and M. Dant, 2019

Market Gardening in Topsham, A. Adcock, 2020

A Home-Grown Business: Pynes of Topsham, M. Patrick and G. Lawrence, 2020

When the Devil Came to Topsham, P. Keen, 2021